CONTENTS

Montjuïc & Raval

Las Ramblas & Barri Gòtic

Port Vell & La Ribera

Spotlight On

Barcelona

Tara Stevens

Written by Tara Stevens
Contributions from Kirsten Foster, Nadia Feddo and Lynne Roberts

Published by AA Publishing, a trading name of Automobile Association Developments Limited, whose registered office is Fanum House, Basing View, Basingstoke, Hampshire, RG21 4EA. Registered number 1878835.

Packaged for Automobile Association Developments Limited by IL&FS, New Delhi

A CIP catalogue record for this book is available from the British Library.

ISBN 978-0-7495-5470-5

The contents of this publication are believed correct at the time of printing. Nevertheless, the publishers cannot be held responsible for any errors or omissions or for changes in the details given in this guide or for the consequences of any reliance on the information provided by the same. Assessments of attractions, hotels, restaurants and so forth are based on the author's own experience and, therefore, descriptions given in this guide necessarily contain an element of subjective opinion which may not reflect the publishers' opinion or dictate a reader's own experience on another occasion. We have tried to ensure accuracy in this guide, but things do change and we would be grateful if readers would advise us of any inaccuracies they may encounter.

Colour separation by KDP
Printed and bound in China by Leo Paper Products

A03233
Maps in this title produced from map data © 1998 – 2005 Navigation Technologies BV. All rights reserved
Transport map © Communicarta Ltd, UK

L'Eixample

Further Afield

Listings

Barcelona

There's a good reason why Barcelona's unofficial biographer, Robert Hughes, dubbed her the "Great Enchantress". Few European cities have so much verve and energy, style or grace, or a better climate. As famous in the 21st century for modern design as it is for Modernisme architecture and medieval streets, not to mention world-class shopping and critically acclaimed food, there are more reasons to visit the Catalan capital than any guidebook can reasonably come up with. But perhaps the most compelling reason of all is to simply roam the city, neighbourhood by neighbourhood, soaking up the sights and the atmosphere as you go.

From its privileged natural position lodged between sea and mountains to the eye-popping, man-made architecture that spans the centuries from the courts of the Catholic kings, from the cathedrals of Gaudí to the sensuously evocative Torre Agbar skyscraper by Jean Nouvel, there is nothing shy about Barcelona. Indeed such is its appeal that the world's leading designers and architects clamour to work here: even now Richard Rogers revamps the abandoned bull ring near the Plaça d'Espanya, while Frank Gehry plots a new train station, La Sagrera, in the style of Gotham city. Nothing ever stands still in Barcelona.

Christened "Barkeno" by the first Iberian settlers (according to legend, the city was founded by Hercules nearly half a century before the building of Rome), then "Barcino" by the Romans, until eventually settling on Barcelona as it is known today, the city has a dramatic 2,000-year-old history and Hughes' book is a good place to start for those who want to delve into the past.

At its peak, the city and its residents were among the most prosperous in Europe and keepers of a mini-empire that included Sicily, Malta, Sardinia, Valencia, the Balearics and parts of Southern France. An outbreak of the plague in the 15th century, however, pretty much crushed all that Barcelona had gained.

Typically resilient, though, the city's second renaissance came in the form of Catalan *Modernisme* at the turn of the 19th century. Keen to flaunt their new-found wealth once trade with America was permitted in 1778 and Spain's Industrial Revolution was well on course to making millionaires of paupers, not to mention their own boom in textiles, the Catalan aristocracy commissioned ostentatious palaces and villas like La Pedrera and the

Casa Batlló, and a new era of the belle epoque was born.

The cash injection of the 1992 Olympics fuelled a third renaissance, and money has been lavished upon the city, sprucing up the famous Gothic quarter, transforming the Born into an area of trendy boutiques and bars, and bringing high-class restaurants into the Eixample. The most recent areas to undergo gentrification are the quiet neighbourhood of Poble Sec and the old fishing quarter of Barceloneta.

Today it is a city that attracts millions of people each year as a long-weekend destination for those visiting from Northern Europe, and a must-see stop on the European itineraries of those coming from across the seas. And then there are those who came and never left. Barcelona's expat population grows by the year.

Gastronomy has played a major role in putting the city on the map, with legendary chefs such as Ferran Adrià being voted the best chef in the world several times over by various high-profile publications, making Barcelona a destination for food-lovers. It even surpasses Paris as a do-before-you-die kind of experience. The city is literally bursting with restaurants and tapas bars that are chewed over and digested by the world's leading food critics, before being proclaimed brilliant.

And the nightlife, while not quite New York, is nevertheless legendary among partygoers. The summer sees the city become a hub of live music festivals, ranging from the stellar electronic festival, Sonar, to Indie Rock Fest Summercase, and free opera recitals in the shaded courtyards of the Barri Gòtic.

Add to this a population with an almost unparalleled lust for life, and if you learn only one thing from your visit it will be to remind yourself: life is for living!

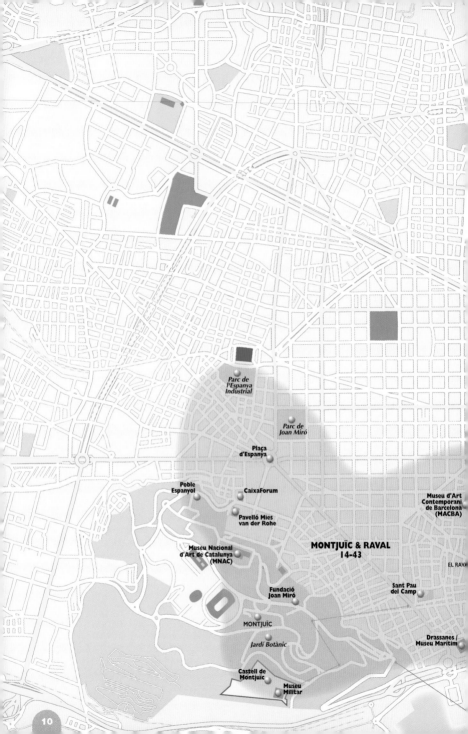

Parc de
l'Espanya
Industrial

Parc de
Joan Miró

Plaça
d'Espanya

Poble
Espanyol

CaixaForum

Pavelló Mies
van der Rohe

Museu d'Art
Contemporani
de Barcelona
(MACBA)

Museu Nacional
d'Art de Catalunya
(MNAC)

MONTJUÏC & RAVAL
14-43

EL RAVA

Sant Pau
del Camp

Fundació
Joan Miró

MONTJUÏC

Drassanes /
Museu Marítim

Jardí Botànic

Castell de
Montjuïc

Museu
Militar

GUIDE TO BOOK REGIONS

0 ————————— 500 m

0 ————————— 500 yds

Parc del Laberint

Parc Güell

GRÀCIA

Hospital
de la Santa
Creu i Sant Pau

**L'EIXAMPLE
110-141**

Museu de
la Música

Casa
Milà

L'EIXAMPLE

La Sagrada
Família

Fundació
ntoni Tàpies

Fundación
Francisco Godia

Manzana de
la Discordia

Museu del
Perfum

*Parc
del Clot*

Plaça de
Catalunya

**LAS RAMBLAS
& BARRI GÒTIC
44-77**

Palau de la
Música Catalana

LAS
AMBLAS

LA RIBERA

BARRI
GÒTIC

Catedral

aça
el Pí

Museu
Frederic Marès

Museu
de la
Xocolata

Plaça de
Sant Jaume

Plaça
del Rei

Plaça
Reial

Museu Tèxtil i
d'Indumentària

Museu Picasso

au
ell

Santa Maria
del Mar

*Parc de la
Ciutadella*

Plaça de
la Mercè

useu
e Cera

*Parc
Zoològic*

PORT VELL

Palau
de Mar

**PORT VELL
& LA RIBERA
78-109**

BARCELONETA

Port
Olímpic

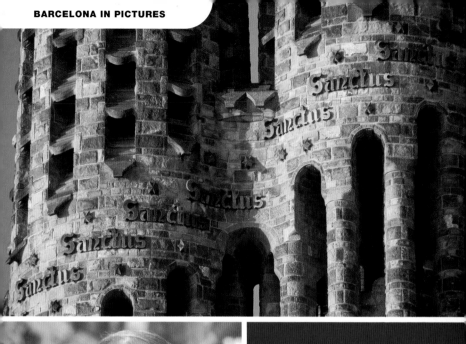

Montjuïc & Raval

Montjuïc, the Jewish Mountain, has a chequered past. The castle, now a popular venue for outdoor film screenings and music festivals in the summer, was once a brutal prison with a gory past. Fast forward a couple of hundred years and it has become a fun military museum complete with suits of armour, and the moat – long since covered over in grass – is a popular venue for outdoor cinema screenings and music festivals. In 1929, Montjuïc was chosen to host the International Exhibition and made headlines again as the site of the 1992 Olympics. The last two decades have seen the region blossom as Barcelona's finest recreational area: a hilly landscape of formal gardens, wide open spaces, world-class art galleries, museums and Olympic sports facilities, as well as offering splendid views of the city.

MONTJUÏC & RAVAL WALK

1. MACBA
See page 30

Starting at the Plaça Universitat, a square between the Gran Vía, the Ronda Sant Antoni and Carrer de Pelai, head down Carrer dels Tallers turning right just past the baroque church of Sant Pere Nolasc and onto Carrer de Valldonzella. This will take you straight out onto Richard Meiers' dashing white cruise ship of a building, the MACBA.

2. Drassanes (Museu Marítim)
See page 20

From here it's a pleasant stroll down Carrer de Joaquín Costa, with its lively bars and across Carrer del Carme onto Carrer de la Riera Baixa. Continue down Rambla del Raval taking in the Moroccan market on Saturdays and straight down Carrer de Sant Oleguer and Avinguda Drassanes. The Museu Marítim is located right at the bottom.

3. Fundació Joan Miró
See page 24

A funicular train on Paral.lel whizzes you up to the top of Montjuïc, affording magnificent views of the city. From here it's an easy walk along sun-dappled parkland to the Joan Miró museum. With nearly 350 of the artist's paintings and sculptures – and a great café – it's a great place for a lunch stop.

4. MNAC
See page 32

Continue along Avinguda de Miramar and head down the hill (there are outdoor escalators if your legs begin to get wobbly) to the newly renovated MNAC, home to an impressive collection of Catalan and religious art, much of which has been reinstated here after being removed from churches and monasteries around the region.

5. CaixaForum
See page 18

After a day of cultural satiation, it's a hop, skip and jump to the Font Màgicà, the magic fountains that dance and light up to various show tunes every 30 minutes from 8pm to midnight in summer. Or come back for that later and finish your tour at CaixaForum with some of the best contemporary art in Barcelona.

A
B
C
D

Mercat Nou

Sants-Estació

Provença

CARRER DE MALLORCA

L'EIXAMPLE

Parc de l'Espanya Industrial

AVINGUDA DE ROMA

CARRER DE VALÈNCIA

CARRER DE VALÈNCIA

TARRAGONA

CARRER DEL CONCELL DE CENT

Hostafrancs

Tarragona

MUNTANER

ARIBAU

BALMES

CARRER D'ARAGÓ

CARRER DE ARAGÓ

D'ENTENÇA

VILLARROEL

Parc de Joan Miró

LA BORDETA

Rocafort

Carrer de Llança de la Diputació

D'URGELL

Rocafort

LES CORTS CATALANES

GRAN VIA DE LES CORTS CATALANES

GRAN VIA DE LES CORTS CATALANES

Plaça d'Espanya

Espanya

COMTE Urgell

Universitat

B-17

Carrer de Sant Fructuós

Carrer de la Guatlla

SEPÚLVEDA

ANTONI

CARRER DE FELAI

CaixaForum

COMILLAS

REINA MARIA CRISTINA

AVINGUDA DE LA

AVINGUDA DE LLEIDA

AVINGUDA DEL PARAL·LEL

CARRER DE FLORODABLANCA

Validonzella

Centre de Cultura Contemporània de Barcelona (CCCB)

Poble Espanyol

MARQUÈS

DEL

Mistral

Tamarit

RONDA DE LA REPÚBLICA

Museu d'Art Contemporani de Barcelona (MACBA)

Pavelló Mies van der Rohe

AVINGUDA DE RIUS I TAULET

Carrer

Mercat del Llibre d'Ocasio & Mercat Sant Antoni

Sant Antoni

Manso

CARRER DEL PINTOR Fortuny

CARME

AVINGUDA

Poble Sec

Parlament

CARRER DEL

Palau de la Virreina

Museu Nacional d'Art de Catalunya (MNAC)

Mirador del Palau

Passeig de les Cascades

RONDA DE SANT PAU

EL RAVAL

4

Montanyans

C de Balx

Museu d'Arqueologia de Catalunya

Liceu

Piscines Bernat Picornell

Museu Etnològic

PASSEIG DE SANTA MADRONA

Carrer de la Creu dels Molers

Gran Teatre del Liceu

L'Anella Olímpica

Sant Pau del Camp

Jardins de Sant Pau del Camp

Plaça Reial

Palau St Jordi

L'ESTADI

Fundació Joan Miró

3

Palau Güell

Museu de Cera

Estadi Olímpic

Carrer dels Tres

AVINGUDA DEL PARAL·LEL

LA RAMBLA

Galeria Olímpica

MONTJUÏC

Avinguda de Miramar

CARRER DEL PORTAL DE SANTA MADRONA

Drassanes / Museu Marítim

2

Jardí Botànic

Doctor Font

Teleféric

DE MIRAMAR

Monument a Colom

Mirador

Miramar

Castell de Montjuïc

Avinguda del Castell

Castell de Montjuïc

PASSEIG DE J CAERNER

Museu Militar

CARRETERA DE MIRAMAR

Maremagnum

0   250 m
0   250 yds

CaixaForum

This castle-like former textile factory shows how *Modernista* architecture transformed the harsh realities of industry into something beautiful. The red-brick building has been stunningly converted into an art museum with a futuristic, airy, glass-fronted entrance, auditorium, bookshop, café and three exhibition spaces. Along with a permanent exhibition of modern art, the museum hosts many varied temporary exhibitions showcasing talent from all corners of the art world.

✚ 17 A2

✉ CaixaForum
Casaromana, Avinguda Marquès de Comillas 6–8

☎ 93 476 8600

🌐 www.fundacio. lacaixa.es

🕐 Tue–Sun 10–8

✋ Free

Ⓜ Espanya

Previous exhibitions have included a massive retrospective of photographer Cartier-Bresson's work and a look at local dress designer Agatha Ruiz de la Prada's crazily creative and flamboyant frocks. The museum can be a little hard to find, tucked away at the base of the Montjuïc hill. From Plaça Espanya walk down the wide boulevard between the Fira de Barcelona's imposing exhibition halls, heading towards the large fountain, then turn right onto Avinguda Rius i Taulet.

Above: Cannons line the walls of one of the courtyards in the Castell de Montjuïc, which has played a role in the city's history

Castell de Montjuïc

Sitting atop Montjuïc, this 18th-century castle is accessible by cable car from the Estació Parc Montjuïc, which connects to the Funicular (cog railway) and has spectacular views of the city.

This former military prison has a long and bloody history. It was here that the former President of Catalunya, Lluís Companys, was executed following his extradition by the Nazis from Paris where he was in exile. Home to political prisoners under General Franco's rule, it also provided a convenient firing line for both Nationalists and Republicans during the civil war. Originally built in 1640 during the War of the Reapers, its present form dates from the 18th century, when it was rebuilt between 1751 and 1799. It now houses a military museum (Museu Militar), with an impressive array of artillery, armour, medals and other military paraphernalia.

Left: View of Montjuïc Castle

✚ **17 B4**

✉ **Castell de Montjuïc**
Parc de Montjuïc,
Carretera de Montjuïc 66

☎ 93 329 8613

🕐 Tue–Sun 10–7

✋ Castell free, Museu Militar
moderate

🚡 Funicular, cable car Parc
de Montjuïc

Drassanes

Established in 1929 as a small museum, the Museu Marítim has grown over the years to become a comprehensive display of Catalan seafaring history, and is one of the finest collections of its kind in the world. It is housed in the Reials Drassanes, an old shipping warehouse dating back to the 13th century, when the Catalan fleet held a powerful influence over many Mediterranean trade routes.

Displays include model ships, nautical instruments, maritime paintings, figureheads and cartography, and date from the earliest examples of shipbuilding in the area to modern freighters. There's also documentary information on the life and work of sailors and fishermen.

Above: Detail of works of art in the Museu Marítim at Drassanes; **left:** A charming restaurant at the museum

✠ **17 D4**

✉ **Drassanes**
Avinguda de les Drassanes s/n

☎ 93 342 9920

🔲 **www.museumaritim
barcelona.com**

🕐 Daily 10–8 (last tickets at 7pm)

💶 Moderate

🚇 Drassanes

Must-sees include a model of *Ictineo*, an early submarine by Narcis Monturiol, and the star attraction – a replica of the royal galley of Juan de Austria. The ship, built in 1568, took Juan into the battle of Lepanto, and this full-scale replica was created to mark the fourth centenary of the event. It is decorated as the original in the style of a floating palace, complete with sound effects and projections which bring it to life.

You'll find that most of the information is in Catalan and Spanish, although good audio guides are available in English.

Above left: One of the finest boats on display in the Museu Marítim; **above right:** From the figurehead collection in the museum; **left:** The museum displays paintings, charts, model ships and boats

Fundació Joan Miró

This homage to Catalan painter and sculptor Joan Miró, regarded as one of Spain's greatest artists, is among Barcelona's best-loved museums and was founded by the artist himself in 1975. Miró's surrealism, abstract forms and primary colours are displayed here with a real sense of his strong Catalan identity. The building itself is a renowned piece of modern design by Miró's friend and architect, Josep Lluis Sert.

Its white walls and terracotta floors contain a permanent collection of more than 11,000 of Miró's tapestries, sculptures, drawings and paintings. Highlights include the *Foundation Tapestry*, created specifically for the museum and the rooftop terrace sculpture garden with 360-degree views of the city.

The foundation library contains around 25,000 books and catalogues, as well as audio-visual resources and journals. The museum hosts regular temporary exhibitions of contemporary art and runs a series of seminars and activities for families and children. There are also musical evenings and guided tours at the weekends.

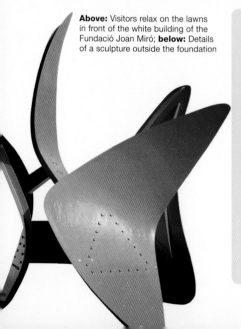

Above: Visitors relax on the lawns in front of the white building of the Fundació Joan Miró; **below:** Details of a sculpture outside the foundation

✙ **17 B3**

✉ **Fundació Joan Miró**
Parc de Montjuïc s/n

☎ 93 443 9470

🌐 **www.bcn.fjmiro.es**

🕐 Tue–Wed and Fri–Sat 10–7 (10–8 Jul–Sep), Thu 10–9:30, Sun 10–2:30

✋ Moderate

🚠 Funicular de Montjuïc

Jardí Botànic

Hidden behind the Olympic Stadium on Montjuïc, this botanical garden is the perfect place to escape the crowds. It's not such a great a place to escape the sun though, as its angular landscaping, with bare concrete and steel and rather sparse planting means it's nothing like a shady, subtropical, foliage-heavy forest.

It's still well worth a visit, though, with the ultra-tidy layout making it easy to find your way around and appreciate each plant or tree, all labelled in English, as well as Latin, Spanish and Catalan. The staff are friendly and helpful and there are great views across the city from the park's high points.

The focus is on flora from Mediterranean-style climates found in Australia, Chile, California, South Africa, the Canary Islands and, of course, the Mediterranean itself. These species make up a quarter of all plant species on Earth and are under serious threat from human activity in their native regions. So catch them here while you still can.

Above: One of the myriad floral varieties found in the Jardí Botànic; **left:** Exotic cactus blooms

✚ **17 B4**

✉ **Jardí Botànic**
Carrer del Doctor Font i Quer 2

☎ 93 426 4935

🌐 **www.jardibotanic.bcn.cat**

🕐 Apr–May and Sep, Mon–Fri 10–6, Sat–Sun 10–8; Jun–Aug, daily 10–8; Oct–Mar, daily 10–5; closed 1 Jan and 25 Dec

✋ Moderate (free last Sun of the month), children under 16 free

Ⓜ Espanya

Montjuïc

Montjuïc is a green and pleasant hill, offering escape from the city's noise and bustle in its myriad parks, galleries and sports complexes. Although it's a centre of leisure today, it has a dark past. The castle on the summit of the hill, now a military museum, was used for centuries as a means of oppressing uprisings and bombarding the citizens below. But today peace reigns in parks such as the Jardins Mossen Costa i Llobera – home to hundreds of cacti. The water features in the Jardíns Laribal offer cool respite from the midday heat, as do the lily pools of Jardíns Cinto Verdaguer, which has lush green grass to stretch out on.

Children are also well catered for in the Poble Espanyol, a rather bizarre reconstruction of a Spanish village, using various architectural styles from across the country. Highbrow culture is on offer in the Museu Etnológic and the Museu d'Arqueologia de Catalunya as well as at the Fundació Joan Miró and the Museu Nacional d'Art de Catalunya – the latter two feature fine restaurants. Montjuïc's most recent claim to fame was as the site of Barcelona's 1992 Olympic games: the Estadí Olímpic and Palau Sant Jordi stadium are being refurbished and are of

limited interest. But the Piscines Bernat Picornell's outdoor swimming pool is great for a dip away from the sea.

Above: The water terraces of the Jardíns Mossen Costa i Llobera

✚ **17 B4**

✉ **Montjuïc**

🚇 Espanya

Museu d'Art Contemporani de Barcelona (MACBA)

Richard Meier's gleaming white geometric building in the heart of the Raval has sometimes been described as a more significant work of art than the collections within. Opened to the public in 1995, MACBA has transformed the surrounding squares in the down-at-heel Raval, now home to a number of cafés, as well as a thriving skateboarding community. Its exhibition spaces lead to a great atrium and are reached by a spectacular series of ramps and glass-floored galleries, which are as awe-inspiring as the works on display.

The permanent collection begins after the civil war, although there are some earlier pieces by Paul Klee and Alexander Calder. It also hosts temporary exhibitions of modern international art, although the lion's share of space is dedicated to Spanish and Catalan work, and exhibitions tend to be somewhat political in context. There's a good shop, with a wide range of books and gifts, as well as a library and cafeteria. The museum conducts lectures, seminars and concerts, and guided tours are available in English on Mondays.

Above left: Exterior of the Museu d'Art Contemporani de Barcelona (MACBA) in the El Raval neighbourhood; **above right:** The spectacular Richard Meier-designed museum

✚ **17 D2**

✉ **Museu d'Art Contemporani de Barcelona (MACBA)**
Plaça dels Àngels 1

☎ 93 412 0810

🌐 **www.macba.es**

🕐 Late Jun–late Sep, Mon–Wed 11–8, Thu–Fri 11am–midnight, Sat 10–8, Sun 10–3; late Sep–late Jun, Mon and Wed–Fri 11–7:30, Sat 10–8, Sun 10–3

✋ Moderate, children under 14 free

Ⓜ Catalunya, Universitat

Museu Nacional d'Art de Catalunya (MNAC)

Catalunya's national art museum sits in an imposing neo-baroque palace – the Palau Nacional – originally constructed for the 1929 Exhibition. Now it houses an enormous collection of art in all its forms: sculpture, painting, drawing, engraving, poster art, photography and even ancient coins, with exhibits spanning the centuries – from the 12th to the 20th.

The museum's heart is in the basement – this elegant vaulted basement plays host to a stunning display of Romanesque religious art that has been rescued from rural Catalan churches. These amazingly vibrant works have been cleverly displayed in reconstructions of the original arched apses where they were found. You won't be able to take your eyes off the hypnotic gaze of the Christ found in the church of Sant Climent de Taüll, from the 12th century.

Although the museum's early and later collections concentrate mainly on Catalan art, its haul of Renaissance and rococo art features Italian and Flemish works, in the Thyssen-Bornemisza and Llegat Cambó collections. Among the more famous names are Luis Cranach, represented by his *Ill-Matched Couple*, a comic painting of a May to December pairing, and Fra Angelico's *Madonna of Humility*, as well as works by Titian, El Greco and Rubens.

✚ **17 A3**

✉ **Museu Nacional d'Art de Catalunya (MNAC)**
Palau Nacional, Parc de Montjuïc

☎ 93 622 0376

🌐 **www.mnac.es**

🕐 Tue–Sat 10–7, Sun 10–2:30

✋ Moderate, valid 2 for days (free first Sun of the month), children under 15 free

Ⓜ Espanya

Above right: The Museu Nacional d'Art de Catalunya (MNAC); **left:** Flagpoles and people outside the museum

Coming to the modern period, the museum focuses on the important *Modernista* movement in Catalan art. One of the most iconic pieces of those times is found here: the mural of painter Ramon Casas and his henchman Pere Romeu on a tandem that used to decorate the wall of the Quatre Gats café. This Parisian-style hangout was the haunt of the top local *Modernista* artists, as well as the young, up-and-coming Pablo Picasso. The *Modernista* period is also explored through design, with a display of furniture from some of the architectural masterpieces of the times, such as the Casa Batlló and the Casa Amatller.

After a recent refurbishment, a fine restaurant has been added to the MNAC's attractions. Oleum is a cut above your average museum café, with elegant table settings and serious service. The dishes, such as quail salad with green apple and rose water, are works of art in themselves. You don't even have to stop admiring the art while you are having lunch – the restaurant has two original works by Catalan modern artist Antoni Tàpies hanging on the walls.

Left: Exterior of the MNAC; **above left and right:** Statues at the Palau Nacional

Parc de L'Espanya Industrial

This futuristic-looking metropolitan space occupies the grounds of an old textile factory just behind Sants train station. While quite different to the more conventional parks of the city, the design by Basque architect Luis Pena Ganchegui is a positive nod to industrialisation. Its features include a man-made lake, several sports areas, fountains and a plaza popular with skateboarders in the afternoons. This social hub is includes a series of striking space-age watchtowers that stand guard at the top of a series of staircases. For those who enjoy urban landscaping this is an absolute gem, with plenty of grassy areas for picnics and lazing about in the sun, dotted with atmospheric statues such as Andrés Nagel's *Dragon without Saint George*. There is a café and even a small play area for younger kids.

Above: Joan Miró's *Woman and Bird – Dona i Ocell*; **left:** The façade of the modern version of the public Roman baths reflected in the water in the Parc de l'Espanya Industrial

Parc de Joan Miró

Sadly, this is an example of what happens when a park isn't cared for properly, though happily it's currently being bulldozed back into shape. Its potential is huge, with its poplar-lined pathways, proud palm trees and wisteria-covered pagodas, although for years it's been largely a dustbowl where kids come for a kick-about and locals walk their dogs. Its also proclaims itself as an impressive outdoor art gallery, boasting Joan Miró's *Woman and Bird – Dona i Ocell* sculpture among others. With Richard Rogers currently working his magic on Las Arenas, the magnificent old, red-brick bullring at one end of the park, and the popularity of the Plaça de Espanya's Feria for trade fairs, the area is undergoing enormous changes, and with luck this park become what it was always intended to be: a pretty, stimulating public space that marries art with nature.

Parc de l'Espanya Industrial

⊞ **17 A1**

✉ **Parc de L'Espanya Industrial**
Plaça dels Països Catalans i Carrer de Muntades

🕓 Open access

✋ Free

🚇 Sants-Estació

Parc de Joan Miró

⊞ **17 B1**

✉ **Parc de Joan Miró**
Carrer de Tarragona

🕓 Open access

✋ Free

🚇 Espanya

Pavelló Mies van der Rohe

This impressive example of modern rationalist architecture was designed by German architect Ludwig Mies van der Rohe, one of the pioneering masters of modern architecture. It was the German national pavilion for the 1929 International Exhibition in Barcelona.

✚ **17 A2**

✉ **Pavelló Mies van der Rohe**
Avinguda Marquès de Comillas s/n

☎ 93 423 4016

🔗 **www.miesbcn.com**

🕐 Daily 10—8, (Wed and Fri closes at 5pm)

🎟 Moderate, children under 18 free

Ⓜ Espanya

Mies van der Rohe's cool, elegant structure uses simple forms and luxurious, expensive materials: glass, steel and four kinds of marble: Roman Travertine, green marble from the Alps, ancient Greek marble and golden Onice marble from the Atlas mountains. The stones' diverse colours and textures add warmth, and the reflections in the pavilion's neighbouring pond give a softening natural effect to an otherwise cold and hard construction.

The curves of the Georg Kolbe sculpture in the pond (another reproduction) also create a contrast to the sharp lines of the building. Mies van der Rohe also designed his iconic Barcelona chair – a simpleL-shaped structure on crossed legs made from leather and steel – to furnish the pavilion. The design is now a classic and is still manufactured and copied.

Above: View of Pavelló Miles van der Rohe – a combination of glass, steel and marble

Plaça d'Espanya

Plaça Espanya's true grandeur is often lost under the smog and noise of heavy traffic. But if you manage to come here late in the evening or on a Sunday, you can appreciate better this impressive, albeit ostentatious, mishmash of architecture.

The centre of the roundabout is a monumental fountain created by Josep Maria Jujol, who also created the wrought iron balconies of Gaudí's La Pedrera building. On one side, the former Las Arenas bullring, with an attractive patterned red-brick façade, has been gutted and is being transformed into a shopping mall by Richard Rogers Architects. But what really grabs your attention, even during rush hour, is the monumental complex of conference buildings that leads from Plaça Espanya to the hill of Montjuïc: two looming Italianate towers mark the gateway to a broad avenue flanked by conference halls and pavilions, some of which were originally built for the 1929 International Exhibition. Follow this boulevard towards Montjuïc and you'll come to the Magic Fountains (Font Màgicà), a spectacular show of dancing water and light. The must-see show takes place every half hour from 8pm to midnight from Thursday to Sunday in summer, and 7pm–9pm Friday and Saturday during the rest of the year.

Above: Details of the "Font Monumental"

✚ 17 B2

✉ **Plaça d'Espanya**

Ⓜ Espanya

Poble Espanyol

An open-air architectural museum, El Poble Espanyol was built in 1929 for the Barcelona International Exhibition. It was intended to last just six months and its permanent status is a testament to its huge success and popular demand. The museum has been open ever since, except during the civil war, when it was used as an internment camp for prisoners.

Traffic-free, and set in the tranquil greenery of Montjuïc, it's a pocket of calm away from the buzz of the city, although it has been dismissed by some as little more than a paid-entry shopping mall. Conceived by Puig i Cadafalch as a model of an architecturally typical Spanish village, it was designed by Francesc Folguera and Ramon Reventós. The pair researched 1,600 towns and villages in the peninsula, along with art critic Miquel Utrillo and the painter Xavier Nogués, before reproducing 117 buildings,

streets and squares to scale. Regions
across Spain are represented in different
architectural styles, from high Gothic to
Mudejar, and the village includes a town
hall, a church, a monastery – which is a
popular wedding venue – and residential
buildings. The main entrance reproduces
the Puerta San Vicente, a 11th-century
gate from the city of Avila; the town hall of
Valdrerobres and the clock tower of Utebo
are also replicated.

Above left: Poble Espanyol; **above right:** A musical performance at Poble Espanyol

✚ **17 A2**

✉ **Poble Espanyol**
Avinguda del Marquès de
Comillas 13

☎ 93 508 6300

🌐 **www.poble-espanyol.com**

🕐 Mon 9–8, Tue–Thu 9am–2am,
Fri 9am–4am, Sat 9am–5am,
Sun 9am–midnight

✋ Moderate, children under 7 free

Ⓜ Espanya

The village was renovated and extended in 1998, and there is a now a strong focus on arts and crafts. Today, the museum contains more than 40 workshops with artists at work displaying traditional crafts, including glass work, ceramics, jewellery, leather, embroidery and basket-weaving. A range of contemporary art is shown across a series of exhibition spaces, including a sculpture garden, and the Fran Daurel Foundation, which contains works from famous international artists as well as Catalan masters such as Dalí, Picasso, Barceló and Tàpies.

There is a wealth of souvenir and trinket shops, along with numerous bars, restaurants, nightclubs and shows. It is a great place for children, with craft workshops, shows, games and story-telling, and guided tours. This was one of the main attractions in the Universal Exposition of 1929. The idea was to gather different types of Spanish architecture under one "roof", to showcase the country's rich cultural variety.

Above: Architectural details of the exterior of Poble Espanyol

Sant Pau del Camp

One of the oldest churches in the city, the Monastery of St Paul in the Field is quite a surprise when you come across it in the middle of the busy, working neighbourhood of Raval.

Its name ("Saint Paul in the Field") stems from the fact that the church was once surrounded by green fields outside the city. Its squat shape and small, tranquil-looking garden with towering palm trees is a reminder of rural Catalunya. No one's quite sure how old it is, but its oldest headstone, that of Guifre II, Count of Barcelona, dates from AD 912. Make sure you see the carvings of flora, fantastical animals and human heads on the façade stone; the pretty garden, with a gorgeous fountain in the church's tranquil cloisters is also a must.

Above: The 12th-century Romanesque church of Sant Pau del Camp towering over the trees at its foot. The church was originally built in a meadow and it still enjoys a little garden setting of its own

- 🕂 **17 D3**

- ✉ **Sant Pau del Camp**
  Carrer de Sant Pau 101

- ☎ 93 441 0001

- 🕐 Tue–Sat 7:30pm–8:45pm, Sun 9:30–1:30

- ✋ Free

- Ⓜ Paral.lel

Las Ramblas &
Barri Gòtic

If there is one street that is synonymous with Barcelona it must be Las Ramblas – the colourful living theatre that provides an artery of cool air cutting up from the sea to Plaça de Catalunya. To stroll the length and breadth of it is a must for any first-time visitor to the city, especially with children in tow. But to get a true feel of the atmosphere of the city you must penetrate the lovely, medieval heart of the Barri Gòtic: a warren of narrow streets, charming plazas and crooked houses overflowing with lush green ferns. Getting pleasantly lost here is all part of its charm, with each layer revealing even more tantalising treasures.

LAS RAMBLAS & BARRI GÒTIC WALK

1. Catedral
See page 52

Start at the Plaça de Catedral for the Catedral. Take the cloister exit onto Crrer de Bisbe – and down Carrer de Sant Sever to the statue of Santa Eulalia in front of the Hotel Neri. Turn right into Plaça Sant Felip Neri with its shoe museum. Head back up the street and go round the cathedral walls anti-clockwise back to Carrer dels Comptes.

2. Museu Frederic Marès
See page 58

Just off here, Plaça Sant Iu is home to Museu Frederic Marès. Stop for a coffee in the charming courtyard, before continuing on up the road to Carrer de la Jaume I. Turn right again and Plaça de Sant Jaume opens up before you, with the Ajuntament (City Hall) on your left and the Palau de la Generalitat on the right.

3. Plaça Reial
See page 70

Continue down Carrer de Ferran past the wacky chocolate emporium Cacao Sampaka on your right, and various souvenir shops. Just before you hit the Ramblas, a small street named Passatge Madoz, flanked by Gaudí's beautiful iron street lamps, opens onto one of the city's finest plazas; great for people-watching.

4. Las Ramblas
See page 74

Exit the plaza on Carrer de Colom, which brings you about one-third of the way up the Ramblas. Soak up the atmosphere on this colourful street: a living theatre of human statues, portrait artists, musicians and flower-sellers. Drop into the Boqueria food market on your left for a fresh seafood lunch at one of the stalls.

5. Plaça del Pí
See page 65

Continue up the Ramblas to Carrer de la Portaferrissa on your right, then continue down Carrer de Petrixol. This street was once full of old *granjas* (dairies) and some remain, serving *churros* and cakes. It's also home to the prestigious art gallery, Sala Pares. Finish at Plaça del Pí with a glass of Catalan champagne.

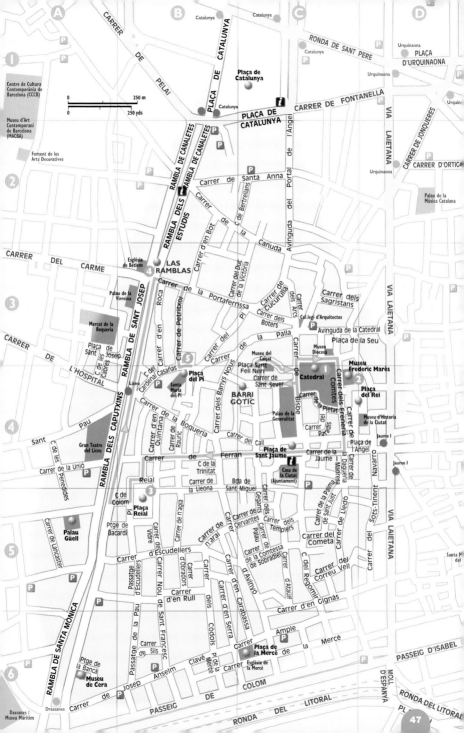

Barri Gòtic

The Gothic Quarter is Barcelona's historic heart. Despite its name, it's not all Gothic, and many of the Gothic-looking features in its narrow streets and historic buildings actually date from the 19th and 20th centuries. The area's origins, however, are even older – this is where the original Roman settlement of Barcino was built.

The Roman centre of town is still the heart of the Barri Gòtic – the Plaça de Sant Jaume, which today is home to the Catalan and Barcelonan local government buildings. Remains of magnificent Roman columns from the Temple of Augustus can be seen in the interior patio of Carrer del Paradis 10, behind the Gothic cathedral, one of the area's true Gothic constructions (at least in part), with beautiful, peaceful cloisters. Peaceful, that is, when the resident half dozen geese aren't creating a ruckus for food! The route of the old city walls, remains of which can still be seen (for example at the bottom of Carrer Baixada Viladecols), roughly traces the outer border of the Barri Gòtic and covers Via Laeitana, Passeig de Colom, La Rambla and Carrer de Fontanella. The part of the Barri Gòtic nearest to the sea has a somewhat rougher air than the more open, modernised, shopping-orientated zone above carrers de Ferran and de la Jaume I. Two of Barcelona's most popular refreshment areas, Plaça Reial and Carrer de la Mercè are here. Both visitors and locals come here to sip wine or cider from the barrel and taste traditional tapas.

The Gothic Quarter probably has Barcelona's highest concentration of bars and restaurants, so if you're not sure where to go for dinner, just wandering the streets should offer you plenty of options. But the Barri Gòtic has more highbrow attractions. In addition to the cathedral, it features many other important examples of religious architecture, from Santa Maria del Pí to the Església de la

Left: A street in the Jewish ghetto of El Call; **above:** A busker entertaining people with a live performance in Plaça Sant Josep Oriol

✠ **47 C4**

✉ **Barri Gòtic**

Ⓜ Liceu, Catalunya, Jaume I

Mercè and the matchbox-sized Capilla de Sant Cristóbal on Carrer del Regomir. The Museu Frederic Marès, behind the cathedral offers a fascinating insight into the everyday objects used in 19th-century society, from cameras to combs. The Col. legi d'Arquitectes de Catalunya on Plaça Nova often holds architectural exhibitions and the Museu d'Història de la Ciutat is a living historic architectural exhibit in itself, comprising some of Barcelona's major medieval buildings, as well as housing some of the city's most important Roman ruins. A more unusual museum can be found in the lovely Plaça de Sant Felip Neri – the Museu del Calçat (shoe musuem) – where you can see the footwear of famous Catalans.

Above: Exterior of a building in Plaça de Sant Just; **below:** The shopfront of Sombrereria on Calle del Call

Left: People sitting outside a café in the Barri Gòtic

Catedral

One of Spain's finest cathedrals, this Gothic masterpiece towers over the heart of the Barri Gòtic and remains a magnet for visitors, with its bell tower, high altar and arches. Officially named Catedral de la Santa Creu i Santa Eulalia, it's affectionately known as "La Seu" after the *plaça* in which it sits, or simply "Catedral".

As a site of worship, the cathedral was predated by a basilica built during the Roman Empire, followed by a mosque and then a 11th-century Romanesque cathedral. Construction on the present building began in 1298, during the reign of Jaume II, when most of the existing structure was demolished. The main building was completed in 1460, with the Gothic façade added in the 19th century and the central

✚ **47 C4**

✉ **Catedral**
Plaça de la Seu s/n, Via Laietana

☎ 93 315 1554

W **www.catedralbcn.org**

🕐 Mon–Fri 8–1:30, 4–7:30, Sat–Sun 8–1:30, 5–7:30

✋ Free

Ⓜ Jaume I

Left: Stone carvings on the front of the cathedral; **above:** A view of the cathedral seen over the rooftops

spire in 1913. Highlights include the tomb of Santa Eulalia, Barcelona's martyred patron saint, which can be found in the crypt. The daughter of a wealthy Barcelona family, Eulalia was crucified by the Roman governor Decius for refusing to denounce her Christian beliefs. Her story, from torture and crucifixion to resurrection, is told in high relief sculptures visible from the front entrance to the cathedral.

The shaded 14th-century cloister also draws visitors, with its central pond and fountain, palm-lined courtyard and its famous white geese. The 13 geese, now reduced to half a dozen, are variously described as each representing a year in the life of Eulalia, or one for each of the tortures she suffered. In legend, they are said to descend from the geese of Rome's Capitoline Hill, who protected the city from attack by the Gauls.

The fountain of St George is worth a visit on Corpus Christi day, for the "L'ou com balla" or "dancing egg", where an egg is placed in the fountain jet. Tradition has it that good fortune will follow in the coming months if the egg does not break.

There are two dozen chapels in all, including the Capilla de Lepanto, which has a 15th-century wooden sculpture of Christ, and the Santa Llucia Chapel – all that remains of the previous Roman structure from which the cathedral was built. Dating from 1268, it can be reached from the cloister and honours St Llucia who also suffered at the hands of Decius, plucking out her own eyes to repel the governor's

Above left: Visitors outside Barcelona Cathedral; **above right:** Detail of the carving on the cathedral

advances. Such was her purity, new eyes miraculously appeared. She is represented over the altar, offering Decius her eyes on a salver.

An elevator takes visitors to the roof for great views of the Gothic quarter (€2.50 per person), and on Sundays at noon you can see Catalans dance the traditional folkloric *Sardana* in front of the cathedral. Evening organ concerts are also held inside throughout the year. Visitors are welcome to attend Mass, held in Spanish and Catalan, hourly on Sundays and throughout the day during the week. During refurbishments visitors invited to "adopt a stone".

Right: Soaring pillars are typical of Catalan Gothic architecture

Museu de Cera

The Barcelona wax museum sits just off Las Ramblas in a neoclassical stately home that belies its unremarkable contents. It's not exactly Madame Tussauds, but it is popular with kids and worth a visit if you have a family to entertain.

The building was designed by aarchitect Elies Rogent. Formerly the site of El Banco de Barcelona, it remains largely intact, complete with winding staircases and frescoes. Features include the "staircase of honour" and "the armoured room", an example of rooms used by banks in the 19th century.

The museum was founded in 1973, the creation of architect and set designer Enrique Alarcon. It shows around 300 wax models of historical figures, celebrities and

literary characters, complete with audio-visual effects. Pope John Paul II hobnobs with the likes of Franco and Hitler, artists and film stars, and horror creations Dracula and Frankenstein.

The museum's café, El Bosc de les Fades (Forest of the Fairies) is next door and a destination in its own right. Fitted out in the style of an enchanted forest, it has gnarled trees, toadstools and a grotto.

Above left: A life-like scene of figures sitting around a table reading, writing and talking; **above right:** A representation of artists at work

✚ **47 A6**

✉ **Museu de Cera**
Passatge de la Banca 7

☎ 93 317 2649

🌐 **www.museocerabcn.com**

🕐 Jul–Sep, daily 10–10; Oct–Jun, Mon–Fri 10–1:30, 4–7:30, Sat, Sun and public holidays 11–2, 4:30–8:30

✋ Moderate

Ⓜ Drassanes

Museu Frederic Marès

Sculptor and collector Frederic Marès i Deulovol donated his home and this fascinating collection to the city of Barcelona. Just behind the cathedral, it is one of the biggest collections of medieval sculpture in the region and is a remarkable repository of objects from everyday life from centuries long gone.

The museum occupies a series of buildings formerly belonging to the Royal Palace and is divided into three sections: sculpture, the collector's cabinet and Marès' library-studio. The palace has beautiful interior courtyards, chiselled stone and soaring ceilings. There is a huge collection of religious sculpture and imagery, from pre-Roman times to the 20th century, but it is the upper floors which contain everyday paraphernalia that really make it worth a visit.

Literally thousands of 19th-century household items and memorabilia, including bicycles, photographs, scissors and clocks are displayed to give a glimpse of life in Barcelona over the years. Objects are organised into themed rooms, including the "Ladies quarter", which shows the life of a 19th-century Spanish woman through a vast collection of bags, hatpins, fans, jewellery and other feminine accessories. The Entertainment Room features toys and automatons. The museum is accessible through an attractive courtyard with an outdoor café, open during the summer months. The café is the perfect resting place during a visit to this incredible museum.

Left: A statue of Mother and Child with cherubs at their feet, set within an ornate niche in the Museu Frederic Marès; **above right:** Visitors leaving through a doorway beneath the sign for the entrance

✚ **47 C4**

✉ **Museu Frederic Marès**
Plaça de Sant Iu 5–6

☎ 93 256 3500

🖥 **www.museumares.bcn.es**

🕐 Tue–Sat 10–7, Sun and public holidays 10–3

✋ Inexpensive (free Wed afternoon and first Sun of the month), children under 16 free

Ⓜ Jaume I

Palau Güell

Commissioned by Eusebi Güell i Bacigalupi, Gaudí's main patron, this was one of the architect's earliest projects and a clear precursor to his later style, featuring his trademark ceramics and parabolic arches. Although relatively nondescript from the front, its playful chimneys rising from the rooftop leave you in no doubt as to its creator.

Built between 1886 and 1889, it connected to the existing Güell family home, and was originally intended to extend to a further property, although plans for this never came to fruition. The Güell family lived here from 1888, and the house featured in the 1888 Universal Exhibition, although it wasn't finished until a year later. The count himself did not stay long, but his daughter, Merce Güell, lived here until 1945, after which it was sold to the provincial government of Barcelona.

Features include intricate wrought-iron gates, elaborately carved wood ceilings, marble columns, marquetry, a flying-bat weather vane and hidden viewing windows high in the walls of the main hall. Worth noticing are the many tricks used to create the illusion of more light, including mirrors, skylights and glass windows over artificial lighting. The entrance shows the parabolic arches that are very important in Gaudí's work, and one of the most interesting parts of the building is the roof with its chimneys. The ornate chimneys that are visible are all distinct and different and are decorated with *trencadis* (broken, coloured tiles). Here, Gothic inspiration alternates with the elegance of Arabic influence.

At the time of writing the palace is closed for repair. It is due to reopen in January 2009. Guided tours will be available in English; however, you might have to put up with long queues.

Above: Chimney pots on the rooftop of Palau Güell

✚ **47 A5**

✉ **Palau Güell**
Carrer Nou de la Rambla 3–5

☎ 93 317 3974

🔲 **www.gaudiallgaudi.com**

🕐 Check website for current times

✋ Moderate

🚇 Drassanes, Liceu

Left: Detail of Gaudí's Palau Güell showing its wrought-iron work

Plaça de Catalunya

Plaça de Catalunya, the meeting point of Barcelona's most important boulevards – the Ramblas, Portal de l'Angel, Rambla de Catalunya and Passeig de Gracia – is the city's hub.

People come to feed the pigeons, groups of South Americans and other immigrants congregate here in the evenings, occasional concerts and events are held, and most visitors will find themselves here at some point during their stay. The main Barcelona tourist board office is located in an underground complex here which houses a booking office, information point, money exchange bureau and souvenir shop.

Shopping is one of the main reasons to end up at the Plaça: one whole side of the square is taken up by the cruise-ship like form of the El Corte Inglés department

store. This is the place to come for things you can't find elsewhere. As well as the usual goods, they have services such as a key-cutter, shoe repairer and dry-cleaner, as well as an exchange bureau and ticket sales stand for local events. The Club del Gourmet food department is the place for those hard-to-find treats from home. There are multilingual signs and information and

translation services. On the opposite side of the Plaça, the Café Zurich is a long-standing popular meeting place for tourists and locals.

Above left: An aerial view of Plaça de Catalunya; **above right:** A beautiful figurine in the central square of Plaça de Catalunya

✚ **47 C1**

✉ Plaça de Catalunya

🚇 Catalunya

Plaça de la Mercè

Although the buildings around it are filled with history, this square is actually a 20th-century creation. Like many other squares in the city, it was made by bulldozing the buildings that used to stand here; the 19th-century fountain originally stood in the port. At the north end stands the basilica that gives the square its name: the Església de la Mercè.

A church was first built here in the 13th century after the Virgin Mary appeared in a dream to a local priest, demanding the creation of a monastic order to pray for the souls of Christians captured by North African pirates. The church that stands today dates from 1775. The Virgin of the Mercy is an important patron saint of Barcelona. The city holds a big fiesta in her honour in September (Festes de la Mercè) and local sports teams come to the church to give thanks when they win any big championship.

The church itself is the only one in the city with a baroque façade and perched on top is a statue of the lady herself, a key feature on the city skyline.

＋ 47 C6

✉ Plaça de Mercè

Ⓠ Drassanes

Above: Inside the busy marketplace on the square

Plaça del Pí

This charming square offers welcome space and light after the tight streets of the Barri Gòtic that wind their way to and from it. These asymmetrical spaces have leafy shaded areas, laid-back cafés and weekend art exhibitions. The Plaça del Pí is dominated by a fine Gothic churche, the Santa María del Pí, with its lovely rose window.

Guitar recitals are often held here in the evenings. Opposite the church is one of Barcelona's most intriguing specialist shops: the Ganiveteria Roca, an old-fashioned knife shop that stocks a tool for every conceivable cutting job. The intricate window displays are a sight in themselves, but the shop is housed in a historic building whose façade is covered in a beautiful example of the sgraffito technique.

A colourful food market is held here every other weekend; producers of organic cheeses, hams, breads and cakes from across Catalunya sell their wares and offer samples to taste. There's more refreshment at café tables under the pine tree that gives the square its name.

Above: The market in Plaça del Pí

🕂 **47 B4**

✉ **Plaça del Pí**

🚇 Liceu

Plaça del Rei

Plaça del Rei is the Gothic heart of the Barri Gòtic. The historic buildings that line this hidden-away square near the cathedral have borne witness to some of Barcelona's most significant events in its early history. In medieval times the square served as a marketplace where hay and flour were sold, but today it is visited by tourists who are drawn by the striking architecture.

Left: A display of colourful wares on Plaça del Rei; **above:** The Museu d'Historia de la Ciutat

+ **47 D4**

✉ **Plaça del Rei**

Ⓜ Jaume I

The Saló Tinell banqueting hall was allegedly where King Ferdinand and Queen Isabella received Columbus on his return from the New World. The Palau del Lloctinent (Lieutenant's Palace), recently renovated, was the local Inquisition headquarters: the condemned were taken away from here to be burned on the Passeig del Born. Many headstones from the Jewish cemetery on Montjuïc were used in its construction, and the Capella de Santa Agata is home to the stone upon which St Agatha's severed breasts were supposedly laid.

The imposing tower with its arched window that looms over one corner of the square is the Mirador de Rei Martí. This was used as a lookout – an early warning system for attacks from the sea and land, and even uprisings by Barcelona's own citizens. These buildings can be visited via the Museu d'Història de la Ciutat, housed in a 15th-century merchant's palace, the Casa Padellas. As with the rest of Barcelona, such historic surroundings can't be left without a modern twist – here the work of Basque artist Eduardo Chillida.

Below: A courtyard within the Plaça del Rei Museu d'Historia de la Ciuat; **right:** The interior of the Capella de Santa Agata, built by Jaume II

Plaça Reial

You can just imagine fine 19th-century ladies in crinolines and gents in top hats wandering the neoclassical arcades of this once grand square, with its giant palm trees, elegant Three Graces fountain and Gaudí-designed wrought-iron lamp posts.

You will need a good imagination because the genteel nature of the Plaça Reial has been rather spoiled by the hordes of boozing backpackers, down-and-outs, bag-snatchers, beggars and buskers that hang out here.

Still, some effort has been made to keep out the worst elements: you'll often find local police parked up here. And it's still a favourite spot with visitors for rest and refreshment after the bustle of the Ramblas, which passes right by the square. Though

most of the bars and restaurants here aren't highly recommended, they're okay for a drink. The Taxidermista restaurant is probably the best option; though Les Quinze Nits draws queues with its no-reservations and low-prices policy, but many don't think it worth the wait. It's at night though, that Plaça Reial has the best to offer (though this is also when it's at its grungiest) in terms of entertainment. The Jamboree and Los Tarantos clubs offer good jazz/blues and flamenco respectively; after the live music both venues join up to host one of Barcelona's liveliest clubs. On the harbour side of the square is Club

13, a Dutch-owned, chi-chi bar, club and restaurant, which attracts a hip 20-something crowd, mostly to its vaulted cellar bar and lively dance floor.

Above: Palm trees in the arcaded oasis of the Plaça Reial

✚ **47 B5**

✉ **Plaça Reial**

Ⓜ Liceu

Plaça de Sant Jaume

This has been Barcelona's "centre" for two thousand years. The Romans built their acropolis here on the small hill they called Mount Taber. The square itself is a fairly recent addition from the 1840s. Previously, a church filled the open space.

The square is the epicentre of the Barri Gòtic. To the north, Carrer de la Jaume I runs to the main thoroughfare of Via Laeitana, to the south Carrer de Ferran heads to the Rambla. Carrer de la Ciutat runs east towards the port and Carrer de Bisbe heads west past the Gothic cathedral. The two very important looking buildings that dominate the *plaça* are the Generalitat (Catalan regional government) building on the cathedral side and the Ajuntament (Barcelona local council) headquarters on the harbour side. The Ajuntament has a neoclassical façade featuring statues of the square's namesake, King Jaume I, and a medieval councillor,

Joan Fiveller. The entrance on Carrer de la Ciutat is a more impressive piece of Gothic architecture, and the Gothic delights continue inside with the Saló de Cent where the Consell de Cent (Council of One Hundred), supposedly Europe's first parliament, sat from the 13th to the 18th centuries. The Ajuntament building is open for visits from 10am to 1:30pm on Sundays. Across the square, the Palau de la Generalitat's Renaissance façade similarly hides a Gothic side entrance. Every second and fourth Sunday of the month, from 10:30am to 1:30pm visitors can take a tour of its treasures, such as the Pati de Tarongers (Orange Tree Patio), and 15th-century Capella de Sant Jordi, featuring pictures and carvings depicting St George's life.

✝ **47 C4**

✉ **Plaça de Sant Jaume**

Ⓖ Jaume I

Above left: Flags fluttering atop the Town Hall in the Plaça de Sant Juame; **above right:** Statues set in niches on the exterior of the Town Hall

Las Ramblas

Las Ramblas or La Rambla? Well, both. This famous mile-long boulevard is five streets in one and each section has its own name. Starting from the Plaça de Catalunya, you'll find the Rambla de Canaletes, so named because of the Font de Canaletes fountain.

It's said whoever drinks from this is sure to return to the city. Next comes the Rambla dels Estudis, named after an ancient university that used to stand here. Now it houses traditional stalls selling birds (even chickens and roosters!) and other small animals, which has led some to dub it the Rambla dels Ocells (birds).

After that comes the Rambla de Sant Josep, nicknamed the Rambla de les Flors. In the 19th century this was the only place in Barcelona where flowers were sold. Its flower stalls still add seasonal colour to the street. At the top of this stretch, to the right, is the Palau de la Virreina, an 18th-century palace that now houses a tourist information centre for culture, ticket sales desk and gallery spaces; its exhibitions are usually well worth a visit. This section of the street also features the world-famous food market, the Boqueria or Mercat de Sant Josep. Crossing through the beautiful wrought-iron and stained-glass archway you hit the front stalls with colourful displays and special packs of fruit and juices made especially for tourists. But beware – you pay a premium for shopping at the front and central aisles. For super-fresh, seasonal, local produce,

Left: A view of Las Ramblas with its tree-lined route clearly delineated as it snakes its way through the city; **above right:** A stone carving of a turbaned man decorates the wall of a building in Las Ramblas

✚ **47 B3**

✉ **Las Ramblas**

⊙ Catalunya (north end), Liceu (central section), Drassanes (south end)

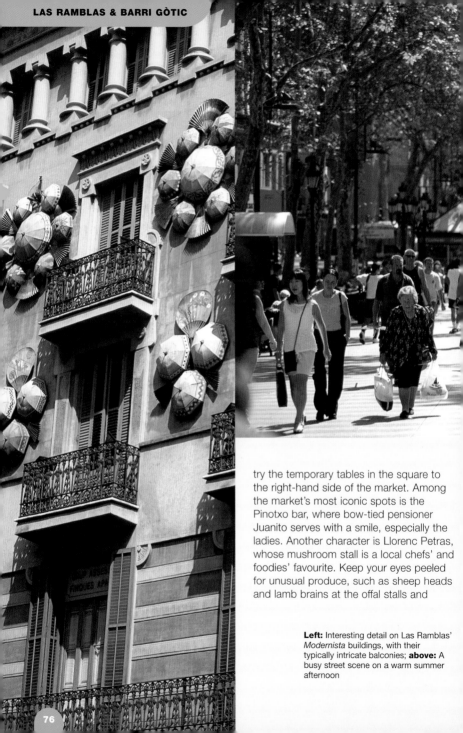

try the temporary tables in the square to the right-hand side of the market. Among the market's most iconic spots is the Pinotxo bar, where bow-tied pensioner Juanito serves with a smile, especially the ladies. Another character is Llorenc Petras, whose mushroom stall is a local chefs' and foodies' favourite. Keep your eyes peeled for unusual produce, such as sheep heads and lamb brains at the offal stalls and

Left: Interesting detail on Las Ramblas' *Modernista* buildings, with their typically intricate balconies; **above:** A busy street scene on a warm summer afternoon

percebes (gooseneck barnacles), which look like turtle feet, among the seafood.

At the end of this stretch of the Rambla look out for the Casa dels Paraigües (House of Umbrellas), with its pretty chinoiserie façade of dragons and umbrellas. The Rambla dels Caputxins (or Rambla del Centre) is the next section of this boulevard. It was the first stretch of the street to be made into a proper promenade for local citizens to take a turn and meet their friends.

Its main attraction is the Gran Teatre del Liceu opera house, rebuilt after a fire in 1994. This highly regarded concert hall features a full programme of great opera and contains an excellent shop and café in a modern annexe. This is also the section of the Ramblas that has the highest concentration of statues.

Finally, the Rambla de Santa Mònica, named after an old convent, runs down to the Columbus statue in the middle of the Plaça Portal de la Pau or Plaça Colom. Here, street artists gather, selling landscapes of Barcelona and caricatures of tourists. Art lovers should visit the Centre d'Art Santa Mònica at the end of the street to the right, for free entry to exhibitions of cutting-edge modern art.

Above: A view of the exterior of the Gran Teatre del Liceu

Port Vell & La Ribera

The neighbourhood of La Ribera is best known for the Born – the southern half of the *barrio* located below Carrer de la Princesa, with its trendy shopping and smart bars and restaurants – while the more residential northern section, Sant Pere, is little explored beyond the Palau de la Música Catalana and more recently the architecturally fabulous Mercat Santa Caterina. As for the rest, there are untold treasures to discover for those who seek them, including the curious El Rey de la Magia magic shop; the smallest door in Barcelona at Carrer del Comerç 10; and the Carrer dels Petons, the kissing street, right next to it.

PORT VELL & LA RIBERA WALK

1. Barceloneta
See page 82

Get off the metro at Barceloneta and walk down Passeig Joan de Borbó. Lined with restaurants, the area is becoming more gentrified. Turn left at the bottom and stroll along the seafront, heading back up into the village along Carrer del Baluard, taking you past the renovated Barceloneta market. Cross the busy roads back into the Born.

2. Museu de la Xocolata
See page 89

Turn right onto the Avinguda del Marquès de l'Argentera and left onto Carrer del Comerç where you'll find a chocolate heaven in the form of the Museu de la Xocolata. The street is also home to some upmarket boutiques and jewellery stores. Halfway along this street is the Passeig del Born on your left.

3. Museu Picasso
See page 86

Just before Santa Maria del Mar, turn right onto Carrer de Montcada where the Museu Picasso occupies several splendid merchants' mansions. Cross over Carrer del Corders and up Carrer d'en Giralt El Pellisser to see the coloured rooftops of Enric Miralles' Mercat de Santa Caterina and continue north to the Palau de la Música Catalana.

4. Palau de la Música Catalana
See page 94

Get your timing right for a tour (9.30am–3pm), or stop at the box office to see if you can get tickets for the evening show. From here, it's a pleasant afternoon ramble along Carrer de Sant Pere Més Alt, finishing up in the Plaça de Sant Pere – a good coffee stop.

5. Parc de la Ciutadella
See page 96

Weave your way through the back streets and down onto the Passeig de Picasso where you'll find the entrance to Barcelona's only inner-city park. Don't forget to pass by the glass conservatory named Hivernacle to check out the evening's entertainment. There's often live jazz here.

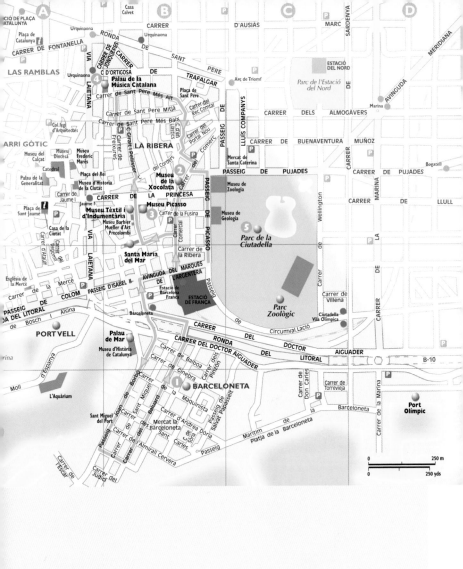

Barceloneta

A triangular shaped jut of land sticking out into the Med, Barceloneta was historically a poor *barrio* of fishermen and factory workers, a shanty town of slum housing on the beach. Then marshland was reclaimed and cheap two-storey buildings put up to house sailors and dock workers.

These homes started small, and overcrowding meant they were divided over and over until the buildings became warrens of tiny apartments, with no running water even right up until the 1960s.

Left: A summer afternoon on the beach at La Barceloneta; **above:** The giant bronze fish sculpture by Frank Gehry

🚑 **81 B4**

✉ **Barceloneta**

🚇 Barceloneta

With cramped conditions indoors, the area's narrow streets became extensions of people's houses, with residents sitting out on the road and treating it like a living room. This street life tradition is continued by today's residents, who are now likely to be beach-loving expats and holidaymakers who turn the *barrio* into party central at the height of summer.

The main access point to the neighbourhood is the Passeig Joan de Borbó, a long boulevard with the marina on one side and a string of seafood restaurants of varying quality (El Suquet de l'Almirall is highly thought of) on the other. This leads down to the beach, which is actually a long succession of eight beaches stretching from the edge of the commercial port all the way to the new Forum complex on the borders of neighbouring Badalona.

At the end of Passeig Joan de Borbó you come to Platja de Sant Miguel, a favourite

with groups of young tourists showing off their tans (or burns) and hanging out at the beach bar *chiringuitos*. The next beach along is the Barceloneta beach proper and is the one used as much by locals as visitors. Its beach-level walkway has new hip bars and restaurants such as the teak-decked Bestial under the boardwalk near the Hotel Arts, and sexy night spots, as well as the domino school where old-timers spend hours at play. There's also a beach library, which lends out books and magazines (some in English) during the busy months of July and August.

Above left: The beach at Barceloneta; **above right:** Sail boats line the deep blue waters; **right:** A sculpture of a crooked tower on the beach by Rebecca Horne

Museu Picasso

One of Barcelona's most visited museums, the Picasso occupies three adjoining medieval palaces, and houses most of the artist's important early works. Although born in Malaga, Picasso's formative years as an artist were spent in Barcelona, and the permanent collection is made up of more than 3,500 works from this period.

The museum opened in 1962, with the majority of the collection being donated by Picasso's lifelong friend Jaume Sabartés. Picasso added some 2,500 of his early works in 1970, including paintings, engravings and drawings, and in 1981 his widow donated a further 141 pieces. You can see childhood sketches and many works from his Rose and Blue periods, but the highlight has to be *Las Meninas*, his series of cubist variations on the masterpiece by Velázquez. Other important works include *Harlequin*, *Woman with Mantilla*, and *Figure with Fruit Dish*. A series of temporary exhibitions focuses on particular aspects of Picasso's work, as well as other avant garde artists.

Far left: The Museu Picasso is housed in medieval mansions; **left:** Modern signage for the museum dedicated to Picasso's work

✚ **81 B2**

✉ **Museu Picasso**
Carrer de Montcada 15–23

☎ 93 256 3000

🌐 **www.museupicasso.bcn.es**

🕐 Tue–Sun 10–8

✋ Moderate, children under 16 free

Ⓜ Arc de Triomf, Liceu, Jaume I

Museu Tèxtil i d'Indumentària

Located opposite the Museu Picasso, Barcelona's textile and clothing museum chronicles the story of fashion and textiles from ancient Egypt to the present day.

The museum is situated in the Palace of the Marquês de Lió, which dates from the late 13th century and still features a small tower and two coffered ceilings from that time. Established in 1982, athe museum has a permanent collection of textiles, clothes and lace, and a programme of temporary exhibitions featuring various designs and styles. It forms part of a group of museums; the others have displays of decorative arts and ceramics, and an admission ticket gets you into all three. This interesting museum is a must-see for a sartorial voyage down the ages.

Right: Beautiful array of antique clothing in the museum

✚ **81 B2**

✉ **Museu Tèxtil i d'Indumentària**
Carrer de Montcada, 12–14

☎ 093 319 7603

🌐 **www.museutextil.bcn.es**

🕐 Tue–Sat 10–6, Sun and public holidays 10–3

💰 Inexpensive, free first Sun of the month

🚇 Jaume I

Museu de la Xocolata

The Museu de la Xocolata is housed in an old convent and covers everything from the discovery of the cocoa bean to how it was ultimately converted into chocolate.

It's also a great place to appreciate the Spanish love of chocolate and it pays homage to the various elaborate and upmarket chocolate makers in the city today. For kids though, the fun is all in the sculptures and if you happen to be in town during Easter, be sure to stop by to admire the "Mona" sculptures of cartoon characters, celebrities and buildings. Tasting is of course all part of the draw, and children and adults alike will delight in the range of chocolate on offer.

Left: The Sagrada Família in chocolate

✚ **81 B2**

✉ **Museu de la Xocolata**
Antic Convent de Sant Augustí, Carrer del Comerç 36

☎ 93 268 7878

🌐 **www.museumdela xocolata.com**

🕐 Mon–Sat 10–7, Sun 10–3

✋ Moderate, children under 7 free

🚇 Jaume I, Arc de Triomf

Palau de Mar (Museu d'Història de Catalunya)

This museum is dedicated to Catalan history, housed in the Palau de Mar, a 19th-century warehouse that is the sole remaining building of Barcelona's old port. Designed in 1881 by engineer Maurici Garràn, the general stores were originally intended as a trading depot.

Regular temporary exhibitions provide a bit of light relief, with insights into political movements and social history in the region. Recent exhibitions have included Somorrostro – a look at the now demolished slums that were home to

dancer Carmen Amaya. There is a library of books, periodicals and catalogues and a shop selling souvenirs and books on the history of Catalonia. The museum café, La Miranda del Museu, is situated on the fourth floor and has an excellent view of

the port. It offers cafeteria service during museum opening hours and restaurant service with a set lunch and à la carte menu in the evenings.

To know more about Catalonia's past you can visit the entertaining Museu d'Història de Catalunya, home to the Museum of Catlan History. Here an array of imaginative exhibits show clearly how this nation within a nation has evolved. Though Catalan history may be something of a mystery to casual visitors, this museum proves that it is definitely worth exploring. The past tells many a tale and at the same time conveys present aspirations. The exhibits are exclusively

Above: The striking façade of the Palau de Mar

✚ **81 B3**

✉ **Palau de Mar (Museu d'Història de Catalunya)**
Plaça de Pau Vila, 3

☎ 93 225 4700

🌐 **www.en.mhcat.net**

🕓 Tue–Sat 10–7, Wed 10–8, Sun and public hoilidays 10–2:30

✋ Moderate, children under 7 free

Ⓜ Barceloneta

in Catalan, but many are self-explanatory and visitors have the option of Spanish and English summaries.

This exciting museum showcases themes from history. Though there are few artefacts on display, the exhibits are truly specatacular. Visitors can work an Arab waterwheel, walk over a skeleton in its shallow grave, climb onto a cavalier's charger, enter a medieval forest and even peer into a primitive stone cabin.

Above: A tree-lined street at Palau de Mar; **left:** Entrance to the Museu d'Història de Catalunya; **far left:** Inside the museum

Palau de la Música Catalana

One of the world's leading concert halls, this spectacular Modernist palace is a UNESCO World Heritage Site. It was built by architect Lluís Domènech i Montaner for the Orfeó Català (Catalan Choral Society) between 1905 and 1908 and is renowned as one of Barcelona's finest buildings. It launched with a season of concerts by the Berlin philharmonic with Richard Strauss, and Pau Casals performed here at the height of his career. Today, it attracts world-class Classical performances and a visit to take in a concert is highly recommended. Tickets can be bought up to one week in advance from the "Les Muses del Palau" shop.

If you can't make it to a concert, it's still worth a trip for a guided tour of the highly decorative interior. Architectural tours run throughout the week in Catalan, Spanish and English. Look out for the mosaic work, high relief and stained glass, Miguel Blay's huge sculpture on the corner of the building, and the columns bearing busts of Bach, Beethoven and Wagner. The main concert hall, which seats 2,000, is illuminated entirely by natural light during daylight hours thanks to the enormous overhead skylight.

✚ 81 B1

✉ **Palau de la Música Catalana**
Carrer de Sant Francesc de Paula 2

☎ 93 295 7200;
Box office: 90 244 2882

🅦 **www.palaumusica.org**

🕐 "Les Muses del Palau" ticket sales
Mon–Sun 9:30–3; guided tours 10–3
(half hourly)

✋ Moderate

🚇 Urquinaona

Above left: Interior of the Palau de la Música; **above right:** The mural-covered concert hall

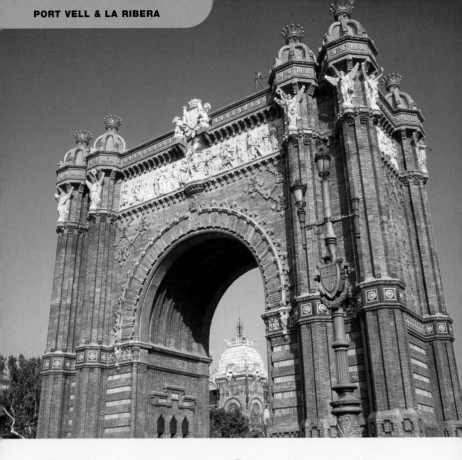

Parc de la Ciutadella

This 30ha (75-acre) park in the centre of Barcelona was created for the purpose of nature, recreation and culture, and is a good place to spend an afternoon, with plenty to see and do.

The landscaped gardens are home to the Barcelona city zoo, the Catalonia Parliament and the museums of zoology, natural history and modern art. There is also a boating lake and large ornamental fountain – The Cascade – co-designed by a young Gaudí.

It occupies the site of an old military fortress, a star-shaped *ciutadella*, built by Philip V in 1716 to protect the city. He

ordered its construction in 1714 during the war of the Spanish Succession after Barcelona fell to him following a lengthy siege. The largest fortress in Europe, it replaced a large swathe of residential buildings in the Ribera district, which were demolished for this purpose. It was partly dismantled under the Junta de Vigilancia in 1841, restored in 1843 and eventually

Above: The broad steps beside the Cascada, created by Josep Fonsere

turned over to the city by Catalan general Joan Prim in 1868.

The area's conversion to a city park began in 1872. It was later designated as a site of the 1888 Universal Exhibition, and several new buildings were constructed, including the Castell dels Tres Dragons, which now houses the Museu de Zoología. The citadel itself was destroyed in 1888, with just the Governor's palace, chapel and arsenal – now home to the Catalan Parliament – left standing.

Above left: The main entrance of the Parc de la Ciutadella is dominated by the Arc de Triomf, a piece of Mudejar-style ceramic brickwork

✚ 81 C2

✉ Parc de la Ciutadella
Passeig de Pujades s/n

◷ Open access

✋ Free

⊕ Arc de Triomf, Barceloneta, Ciutadella

Parc Zoològic

Barcelona's Zoo covers a large area of the Parc de la Ciutadella. Open since 1892, it houses more than 7,500 animals from 400 species.

The zoo has a large collection of endangered primates, including Bornean orang-utans and mangabeys, the world's smallest monkey. Snowflake the Gorilla was the star attraction until his death in 2003. It's also home to big cats, wolves, mammals and a group of bottlenose dolphins, which give daily performances. The Iberian wolf also happens to be a threatened species.

There is a seperate, fun children's section with plenty of activities for kids as well as a restaurant, picnic area, gift shop, electric cars and a miniature train.

Right: The fountain of the "Lady with the umbrella" stands in a pond amidst trees and flowers

✚ **81 C3**

✉ **Parc Zoològic**
Parc de la Ciutadella

☎ 93 225 6780

🌐 **www.zoobarcelona.com**

🕐 Jun–Sep, daily 10–7;
Mar–May and Oct, 10–6;
Nov–Feb, 10–5

✋ Expensive

🚇 Ciutadella

Port Olímpic

Port Olímpic was built in 1988 to host the 1992 Olympic Games and became the success story of the Nova Icaria project. Designed by architect Oriol Bohigas on formerly contaminated industrial land, this once wasted space was reinvented as a 700-berth marina and thriving waterfront community.

It's now a somewhat tacky entertainment and leisure mecca with a wide selection of bars, nightclubs, shops and restaurants. You can rent speedboats for tours of the port, and sailing, windsurfing and other

Above: The imposing twin towers at Port Olímpic

🏠 **81 D4**

✉️ **Port Olímpic**

🚇 Ciutadella

water sports are readily available. If you're looking for it, you can't miss it. It has two unmissable landmarks: the twin towers of the Hotel Arts and Mapfre Tower, which are visible from all of Barcelona's lookout viewpoints. The promenade here is a wide walkway which links the Icaria and Barceloneta beaches, on either side of the Port Olímpic. A further unmistakable landmark is Frank Gehry's *Peix D'Or* (Golden Fish), the giant bendy, bronze, lattice-work structure that looms beneath the Hotel Arts and which is only really recognisable from a distance. Rumour has it that it's facing the opposite way to the architect's original intentions. Apparently the hotel didn't want its guests gazing up a fish's backside, although you may wonder how they could tell which end was which. There's a casino next door to the hotel.

The port is also the home to the infamous Baja Beach Club. As well as being known for its tanned cocktail waiters and waitresses, this young and lively club is also

famous for introducing a chip system for its regulars. The club's clients can choose to have a microchip inserted in their arm which gives them speedy entry to the club and service at the bar – they're just swiped like a tin of beans at the supermarket checkout!

Nearby Barceloneta offers some good seafood restaurants and the dark, narrow streets are a contrast to the bright commercialism of the port. The old fisherman's quarter was built in the 18th century to house residents from the parts of the Ribera demolished to make way for the Ciutadella.

The beach can get pretty crowded in the summer (Icaria less so), but you can still get a reasonable amount of personal space. There is always something going on, and it's a good spot to relax and people-watch.

Above: Boats in the marina, which is the heart of the Olímpic district

Port Vell

Like the Port Olímpic, Port Vell is a triumph of urban renewal. This was a run-down industrial site before the 1992 Olympics, but the area has since been transformed into a thriving harbour filled with yachts and is lined by restaurants, bars and tourist attractions.

Previously a mass of docks and warehouses that blocked access to the sea, the port now connects the city to the Mediterranean via the Moll de Fusta, a system of walkways and streets that separates pedestrians and vehicles into different layers. As part of the area's regeneration, the coastal road was moved underground, and a promenade now runs from the Columbus monument to Barceloneta. From the commercial port near the Montjuïc hill, a landscaped walkway runs alongside the water, passing the landing stage for the Golondrina

pleasure boats, which take trips out of the harbour and up the coast.

It leads to a graceful walkway, with a low bridge that opens to let the boats pass, which guides you to the Maremagnum complex. After a recent refurbishment, this mall is now a rejuvenated hot spot, featuring open-air concerts, wine-tasting fairs and hip fashion markets. It also houses an IMAX cinema, a huge selection of shops and restaurants and Barcelona's Aquarium. This is home to 11,000 fish, arranged by themed habitats. The highlight is an underwater viewing tunnel through which you can observe many species, such as sharks gliding over your head. There are special activities for kids, including a touch tank where they can get close up and personal with rays and other sea creatures.

✚ **81 A3**

✉ **Port Vell**

Ⓜ Barceloneta

Above: Watching the sharks from the underwater tunnel at the Aquarium

Back on the mainland, the promenade passes the Museu Marítim's schooner *Santa Eulàlia*, which dates from 1918. This historic vessel was completely restored in 1998 and is now a fully working ship. It can be visited with a museum entry ticket. You can also see a replica of *Ictineo II*, one of the world's earliest submarines, invented by Catalan Narcis Monturiol.

This whole area was once filled with dockside bars and restaurants. Now the only relic is Javier Mariscal's strange fibreglass lobster or crayfish (no one seems able to decide what it is) on the roof of the former seafood restaurant Gambrinus, now just a shell. A strange colourful sculpture, Roy Lichtenstein's *El Cap de Barcelona* (Head of Barcelona)

towers above the entrance to the Palau del Mar area, opposite the pleasure marina. The Palau del Mar, an imposing former warehouse, is now home to the Catalan History Museum and a number of popular terrace seafood restaurants.

If you have a head for heights, you can get a great aerial view of the whole area and the rest of the city by taking a cable-car ride from the Torre San Sebastia, just behind the San Sebastia beach, to the hill of Montjuïc.

Above left: Dining in Port Vell; **above right:** View from the Monument a Colom over the harbour at Port Vell; **right:** Boats in the harbour

Santa Maria del Mar

The simple elegance of this medieval basilica makes it one of the most striking buildings in Barcelona. It is an outstanding example of the Catalan Gothic style, and provides a spectacular contrast to the more complex creations of later Gothic and Modernist buildings in the city.

It's a breathtaking space characterised by clean horizontal lines and large bare surfaces. Built with unusual speed for a medieval building, it was constructed between 1329 and 1384 as Santa Maria de les Arenes and later renamed. It was designed by a stonemason, Berenguer de Montagut, and built by the people of the Ribera. Popularly regarded as the "people's church", it is the city's most popular spot for weddings, and retains the calm air of a functioning place of worship rather than a tourist attraction.

Named for St Mary of the Sea, it was intended to bless and protect the Catalan fleet, and the first stone was laid to commemorate the conquest of Sardinia.

Seafarers of all types are included under the lady's patronage, and it was common for sailors to visit the church to pray before heading to sea.

It's splendid features are accentuated by a lack of clutter that owes a debt to the anti-clerical anarchists who attacked and burned the building in July 1936. Part of the Barcelona uprising, the attack came upon the eve of the civil war. The basilica burned for 11 days and was almost destroyed,

Above left: Inside the church of Santa Maria del Mar; **above right:** The impressive façade of the church

✚ **81 B3**

✉ **Santa Maria del Mar**
Plaça de Santa Maria

☎ 93 310 2390

🌐 **www.bcn.es**

🕐 Mon–Sat 9–1:30, Sun and public holidays 10–1:30, 4:30–8

✋ Free

🚇 Jaume I

JOSEP·ORIOL   S·IGNASI·DE·LOYOLA   S·SALVADO

leaving it devoid of the multitude of baroque images that are found in many Spanish churches. It was restored at the end of the civil war by Bauhaus-trained architects, with a renewed attention to simplicity of lines.

Inside, the soaring columns of the main nave give rise to high fan vaults. Paintings on overhead keystones represent scenes including the *Coronation of the Virgin*, the Nativity, the Annunciation and the Barcelona coat of arms. There are 34 chapels dedicated to different saints and images, including Eulalia, who was originally laid to rest here before being taken to her final resting place at the cathedral.

A huge stained-glass rose window dates from the 15th century. The original was built earlier, but was destroyed during an earthquake in which 25 people were killed and dozens injured.

The church hosts regular concerts which make excellent use of its superb acoustics. Medieval music scores were written to accommodate a six-second acoustic delay characteristic of large spaces, and it's a wonderful place to hear such early music. Particularly worth coming to are Handel's *Messiah* at Christmas and Mozart's *Requiem* at Easter.

Above left: The carved façade of Santa Maria del Mar; **above right:** A close view of a statue outside the church; **left:** Details of the stained-glass windows, which date from the 15th century

L'Eixample

The seat of Modernism in Barcelona, L'Eixample, or "extension", forms a sprawling grid-system of apartment blocks around the old city. With its distinctive bevelled block corners, delightful architecture and top-class restaurants, it's an area well worth exploring. Split down Carrer de Balmes into L'Eixample Esquerra (left) and Dreta (right), the latter is the most rewarding in terms of A-list buildings such as Gaudí's La Pedrera (Casa Milà) and Casa Batlló as well as other *Modernista* greats. The tree-lined boulevards with their numerous pavement cafés make for great people-watching, while Passeig de Gràcia itself, the central artery of L'Eixample, is Barcelona's very own Fifth Avenue.

L'EIXAMPLE WALK

1. Plaça de Catalunya (page 62)

When the city walls were demolished in the 19th century, a gap was left, separating the old city from the new. Covered over with concrete and planted with a few token trees, what is now Plaça de Catalunya lacks grandeur as a central city plaza, but serves as a central landmark. Café Zurich is a popular meeting spot on the west side of the square, while El Corte Inglés department store dominates the east.

2. Manzana de la Discordia
See page 124

Stroll northwards along Passeig de Gràcia – a glamorous boulevard that houses most of Barcelona's designer stores – taking in the whimsical Museu del Perfum, and on up to the illustrious Manzana de la Discordia where three of the city's most eye-popping examples of Modernist architecture vie for attention.

3. Casa Milà
See page 114

Continue north to Antoni Gaudí's fabulous apartment block, Casa Milà. The Hotel Omm around the corner on Carrer del Rosselló is a modern interpretation of Gaudí's work and it's interesting to compare the two. Don't forget to look down. As well as Gaudí's paving stones, Passeig de Gràcia also has 31 modernist benches and lamp posts.

4. Gràcia
See page 120

Continue northwards across Avinguda Diagonal and wend your way up into Gràcia. Its charming narrow streets (many of which are becoming pedestrianised), numerous small plazas, two markets and interesting shops give it a quaint, bohemian atmosphere.

5. Parc Güell
See page 130

Further northwards, a steep climb to Carrer del Torrent de les Flors and up Carrer de Larrard leads to Gaudí's magical, mystical Parc Güell. Declared a UNESCO site in 1984 for its brilliant fairy-tale ambience, the park affords spectacular views of the city, especially if you get away from the crowds and go up to Parc del Carmel.

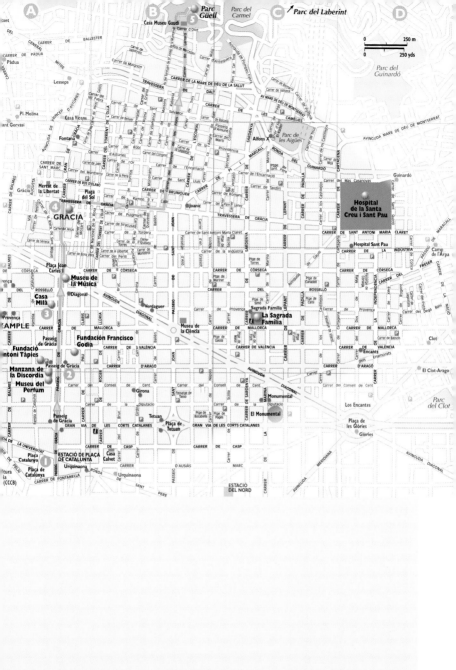

Casa Milà

Casa Milá, more commonly known as La Pedrera (The Quarry), was Gaudí's last secular design, and his largest civil building. It was commissioned as an apartment block by Pere Mila i Camps, a wealthy developer impressed by the Casa Batlló, which Gaudí had recently completed. Constructed between 1906 and 1910, it was not very well-received by the public when it was built.

Above: A fascinating array of uniquely styled chimneys on the rooftop of Gaudí's Casa Milà

As you'd expect from Gaudí, it's a fanciful affair. The undulating exterior walls, built from Montjuïc limestone, are reminiscent of the ocean, and its doors and windows appear to be dug out of sand. There are no straight lines or right angles, inside or out, and no load bearing walls. The building rests on pillars and arches, with apartments of irregular shape and size arranged around two central courtyards.

The exterior is decorated with intricate balconies covered with seaweed-like wrought-iron foliage, created by Josep Maria Jujol. It was originally intended to honour the Virgin Mary, and be adorned

✚ **113 A3**

✉ **Casa Milà**
Passeig de Gràcia 92

☎ 93 484 5900

🌐 **www.casa-mila.com**

🕐 Daily 10–8 (English tours Mon–Fri at 6pm)

✋ Moderate, children under 12 free

Ⓜ Diagonal

with her statue, but the initial design was altered by Milà, who thought better of it following the anti-religious violence of the Setmana Tràgica (Tragic Week) of 1909. Fearing that the house would be mistaken for a convent or church, the Milàs eliminated all religious imagery.

Milà's wife was not a fan of the architect, and following Gaudís death in 1926 she transformed the main floor of Casa Milà into conventional rooms in the style of Louis XVI.

The spectacular roof terrace is the building's main attraction. It sports

Left: One of the curvacious roof chimneys

groups of surrealist chimney stacks on an undulating surface that give it a distinctly lunar appearance. The chimneys were nicknamed *espantabruxes* (witch-scarers) and have variously been interpreted as veiled Saharan women or helmeted warriors. The roof has outstanding views of the neighbourhood, and a bench similar to the one in Park Güell.

The building was designated a UNESCO World Heritage Site in 1984 and it's now owned by the Caixa de Catalunya. Some apartments are privately owned, but the top floor, attic and roof are open to visitors. It includes a cultural centre with a wealth of information about Gaudí. After restoration in 1996, the Espai Gaudí was added to the attic. It's an excellent resource on the architect, with photographs and scale models of many works, along with explanatory notes.

The Pis de la Pedrera apartment was also added at this time, to provide a glimpse into the life of a typical resident family in the early 20th century. The entire first floor is now an exhibition space, and jazz and flamenco concerts are held on the roof in the summer.

Above left: A grand staircase inside Casa Milà; **above right:** The undulating exterior

Fundació Antoni Tàpies

Antoni Tàpies is a Barcelona-born modern artist, who set up this eponymous foundation in 1984 as a space for celebrating contemporary art. His most iconic works incorporate unusual materials, such as sand, clay and marble dust, and feature distinctive, repeated graphic emblems.

✚ **113 A3**

✉ **Fundació Antoni Tàpies**
Carrer d'Aragó 255

☎ 93 487 0315

🌐 **www.fundaciotapies.org**

🕐 Tue–Sun 10–8

✋ Moderate, free 18 May and 24 Sep

🚇 Passeig de Gràcia

Most of the Fundació's exhibition space is given over to a rotating display of Tàpies' own works, from early examples linked to the Art Brut and surrealist movements to his most famous works – the "Matter" paintings, which he started to work on in the 1950s. The space is also used for temporary exhibitions of work by other artists, lectures, conferences and films. Even if you don't go in, you can see an example of Tàpies' art from the street. *Núvol i Cadira* (Cloud and Chair) is a tangled web of piping and metal net, sitting on the building's roof.

Above: A view of the building's rooftop with its piping and metal net

Fundación Francisco Godia

Francisco Godia was a Formula One driver in the 1950s. He combined a love of art with a head for business and a passion for motor racing. When he wasn't driving fast ("the most wonderful thing in the world"), he showed exquisite taste and great artistic sensibility as a collector.

The money Godia earned from racing enabled him to amass an amazing private art collection. He aquired work by some of the most important artists of the 20th century. Ceramics enthusiasts will love exploring the Fundación's amazing range of Spanish ceramics ranging from medieval pieces to modern artistic creations. There's also an important display of religious art, particularly Romanesque sculptures. Lovers of more modern art should check out paintings by Ramon Casas, a celebrated Catalan painter of the *Modernista* period, who was a mentor to the young Picasso.

Above: Exhibit at the Fundación Francisco Godia

✚ 113 A3

✉ **Fundación Francisco Godia**
Carrer de València 284 pral

☎ 93 272 3180

🌐 www.fundacionfgodia.org

🕐 Mon and Wed–Sat 10–2, 4–7, Sun 10–2; guided tours Sat and Sun at noon

✋ Moderate, children under 5 free

Ⓜ Passeig de Gràcia

Gràcia

This neighbourhood at the top of the Passeig de Gràcia used to be a separate town and it still maintains a very different feel to the rest of Barcelona. Its low buildings, narrow streets and plentiful squares give it a cosy, relaxed feel that reflects the family-orientated and alternative lifestyles of most of its inhabitants.

Popular as a place for students to live, it used to be a real party *barrio*, particularly around the Plaça del Sol, but recent efforts by the authorities have clamped down on late-night noise. However, there are still plenty of bars catering mostly for the student crowd, whether of the hip or the hippy persuasion. There are lots of good places to eat here at reasonable prices, offering a range of cuisines from

Catalan to Mexican, Persian, Italian and even Ethiopian.

Gràcia also has two of the few cinemas, Verdi and Verdi Park, in Barcelona that show non-dubbed films. But the zone's biggest claim to fame is its Festa Major held over the third week in August. Each street is decorated by the residents, according to a theme. In some cases these decorations are amazing creations worthy of Hollywood craftshops: giant papier mâché aliens crawl up the sides of buildings and whole streets

are transformed into alternative worlds. All the traditional elements of local festivals are here: drinking, dancing, music and general mayhem and merrymaking, with everyone partying all night, from grannies to babes-in-arms.

Above: An afternoon scene that reflects the relaxed lifestlye of the inhabitants

✚ **113 A2**

✉ **Gràcia**

◉ Diagonal, Fontana, Joanic, Plaça Molina

Hospital de la Santa Creu i Sant Pau

The original Hospital de la Santa Creu was formed in 1401 with the merger of six small medieval hospitals. But the current building dates from the 1900s, when a new hospital was needed to cope with the demands of an increased population and advances in medicine.

Local banker Pau Gil provided the money for construction, and the name of the hospital had Sant Pau added in his honour. The famous *Modernista* architect Lluis Domènech i Montaner was charged with the design of the building. The first stone was laid in 1902 and the final touches were made in 1930. In 1997 it was awarded the status of World Heritage Site by UNESCO.

The design consists of 18 pavilions connected by underground tunnels, set at a 45-degree angle to the rest of the Eixample's grid system, to get more sunlight. The red-brick, tile and carved-stone buildings feature Moorish arched windows, Byzantine columns, colourful mosaics and murals, carved angels and flowers, all intended to help patients' recovery by giving them beautiful surroundings. However, despite its good intentions, the building's age and design don't seem compatible with today's medical needs and a new, modern, rather less inspirational building at the corner of the complex will eventually house all the patients, leaving Domènech i Montaner's masterpiece to be used for education and research (and tourism) purposes.

✚ **113 D2**

✉ **Hospital de la Santa Creu i Sant Pau**
Carrer de Sant Antoni Maria Claret 167

☎ 93 291 9000

🌐 **www.santpau.es**

🕐 Daily 10–2, guided tours in English daily at 10:15am and 12:15pm

✋ Inexpensive

🚇 Hospital de Sant Pau

Left: The entrance of the Hospital de la Santa Creu i de Sant Pau; **above:** A cross on the hospital gates

Manzana de la Discordia

The Block of Discord (a pun on the apple of discord of Greek myth – *manzana* means both apple and block in Spanish) is a set of three neighbouring buildings on the Passeig de Gràcia, each of which represents a masterpiece by one of the three top *Modernista* architects: Gaudí, Puig i Cadafalch and Domènech i Montaner.

The first as you head away from Plaça de Catalunya is the Casa Lleó-Morera by Lluís Domènech i Montaner, on the corner of Carrer del Consell de Cent. Although it was a revamp of a previous structure, rather than a totally new building, this project still won Domènech I Montaner the Ajuntament's first architectural prize. Unusually, the name of the building comes not from its owner but its architectural motifs – the lion and the mulberry, which Domènech i Montaner took from medieval coats of arms. Other motifs on the façade include the lightbulb and telephone – both recent inventions at the time of its construction. Its Gothic feel is said to have been inspired by the works of Wagner, who was the favourite composer of Catalan worthies during the *Modernista* period.

Next along is Josep Puig i Cadafalch's Casa Amatller, another remodelling job. Commissioned by the chocolate magnate Antoni Amatller, its Flemish-influenced stepped gable gives it a suitably Hansel and Gretel gingerbread house look. The intricately carved stonework and wrought-iron balconies show Gothic and baroque influences, all adding up to a typically Modernist mishmash of styles. The ground floor houses the grand and historic Catalan

Left and above: The glittering, coloured façade of Antoni Gaudí's Casa Batlló, coverd with *trencadis* (pieces of broken ceramics)

✚ **113 A3**

✉ **Manzana de la Discordia**
Casa Lleó-Morera, Passeig de Gràcia 35; Casa Amatller, Passeig de Gràcia 41; Casa Batlló, Passeig de Gràcia 43

☎ 93 216 0306

🌐 **www.casabatllo.es**

🕐 Casa Batlló: daily 9–8

✋ Expensive, children under 6 free

🚇 Passeig de Gràcia

jeweller Bagues – its shop windows are the originals, with ornately carved floral motifs in stone.

Finally, there's Antoní Gaudí's Casa Batlló next door. Again, this was a refurbishment commission, from the Batlló family who'd made their money from textiles. Gaudí is said to have been aiming for a "vision of paradise" with this work, though many contemporary commentators thought it more a vision of horror. The most distinctive part of the building is its frontage, completely covered in ceramic tile mosaics, though these were actually the work of Gaudí's ceramicist, Josep Maria Jujol, whose genius is often overshadowed by that of his more famous master. Gaudí's other iconic materials and techniques are

also here – twisted wrought iron in fantastic shapes on the balconies, stone seeming to come alive and take organic form and glass is coloured to create works of art with light. Some say the shapes of the façade suggest St George's fight against the dragon. There seems to be not a single straight line in the building, which allegedly caused concern to Señora Batlló because there was nowhere to fit her daughter's piano. Gaudí's reaction was simply to suggest that they forget the piano and buy a violin instead.

Above: The Manzana de la Discordia buildings on Passeig de Gràcia; **right:** Architectural details of a Manzana de la Discordia building

Museu de la Música

Based in the L'Auditori concert hall, this collection of musical instruments and documents hopes to inspire people and to deepen the public's understanding of music. It's aimed at everyone, not just musicians or the musically minded.

✚ **113 A3**

✉ **Museu de la Música**
Carrer de Padilla 155

☎ 093 256 3650

🌐 **www.museumusica.bcn.es**

🕐 Mon, Wed–Fri 11–9, Sat–Sun 10–7

✋ Inexpensive, children under 16 and OAPS free

🚇 Marina

The exhibition uses its displays of instruments, archives and objects to illustrate the history of music in Catalunya through the ages. Starting with music from ancient civilisations it leads to the birth and spread of polyphonic music, the baroque, Classical and Romantic periods, the music industry in the 19th century and the new styles in the 20th century. Another exhibit looks at the various ways of "recording" music throughout history, from writing it down to the sophisticated recording techniques in use today. Kids will enjoy the exciting interactive room, where the question "Why sound?" is posed.

Above: A music score from the Museu de la Música

Museu del Perfum

Most museums these days have a shop, but this is a shop that has a museum. The Perfume Museum sits in a back room of the Regia cosmetics store. It houses a collection of almost 5,000 perfume bottles, jars and other beauty-related items, such as old advertising material.

The collection includes examples from Ancient Greece, Rome and Egypt as well as Etruscan and Arab artefacts. Perfume has always been a highly valued commodity throughout the ages and the containers used to hold it have reflected this; some are exquisite works of art, made from materials as expensive as their contents.

The museum is divided into two parts: the first displays the ancient bottles, according to chronological order, and the second shows modern perfumes according to brand.

Above: A display of some of the famous brands at the Perfume Museum

✚ **113 A4**

✉ **Museu del Perfum**
Passeig de Gràcia 39

☎ 93 216 0121

🌐 **www.museodelperfum.
com**

🕐 Mon–Fri 10:30–1:30,
4:30–8, Sat 10:30–2

✋ Inexpensive

Ⓜ Passeig de Gràcia

Parc Güell

One of the most enjoyable and affordable (it's free!) of Gaudí's Barcelona masterpieces, Park Güell gets very crowded at peak time. But despite this, it's always breathtaking, both in terms of its views of the city and examples of Gaudí's almost unnatural talent.

The park's fairy-tale feel is reinforced as soon as you step through the main gates: the mushroom-roofed gatehouses were based on designs for the opera *Hansel and Gretel*. From here a stone staircase decorated by a mosaic-covered salamander leads to a cool, echoing, vaulted space, where Gaudí's mastery of stone is displayed in the organic-looking palm tree-shaped pillars. The next level brings you to the esplanade, edged by an

✚ **113 B1**

✉ **Parc Güell**
Carrer d'Olot

☎ Museum: 93 219 3811

🌐 **www.casamuseugaudi.org**

🕐 Park daily 10am–sunset; Museum Apr–Sep, daily 10–8; Oct–Mar, 10–6

✋ Park free; museum moderate

🚇 Lesseps

Left: Trees line the entrance wall of the Parc Güell; **above:** The delightful Parc Güell with its fairy-tale feel

131

immense curving concrete bench covered with colourful broken tiles, with a fantastic panaorama of Barcelona and the sea. Escape the crowds by climbing to the highest reaches of the park, where winding paths lead to hidden benches sitting beneath cherry trees. The best way to get to the park is the No 24 bus – it's a long steep walk from the métro.

Above left: The walls of Parc Güell with their ceramic lettering; **above right:** One of the surreal creations in Gaudí's Parc Güell

A ceramic serpent, or perhaps it's a dragon, slithers down the stairway towards the main entrance guarded by two gingerbread-style buildings that must be among the oddest creations found here.

Surrealist Salvadore Dalí was filled with "unforgettable anguish", as he strolled among the uncanny architectural forms of this hilltop park, Antonio Gaudí's extraordinary piece of landscape design.

Right: Sala Hipóstila, also known as the Hall of 100 Columns

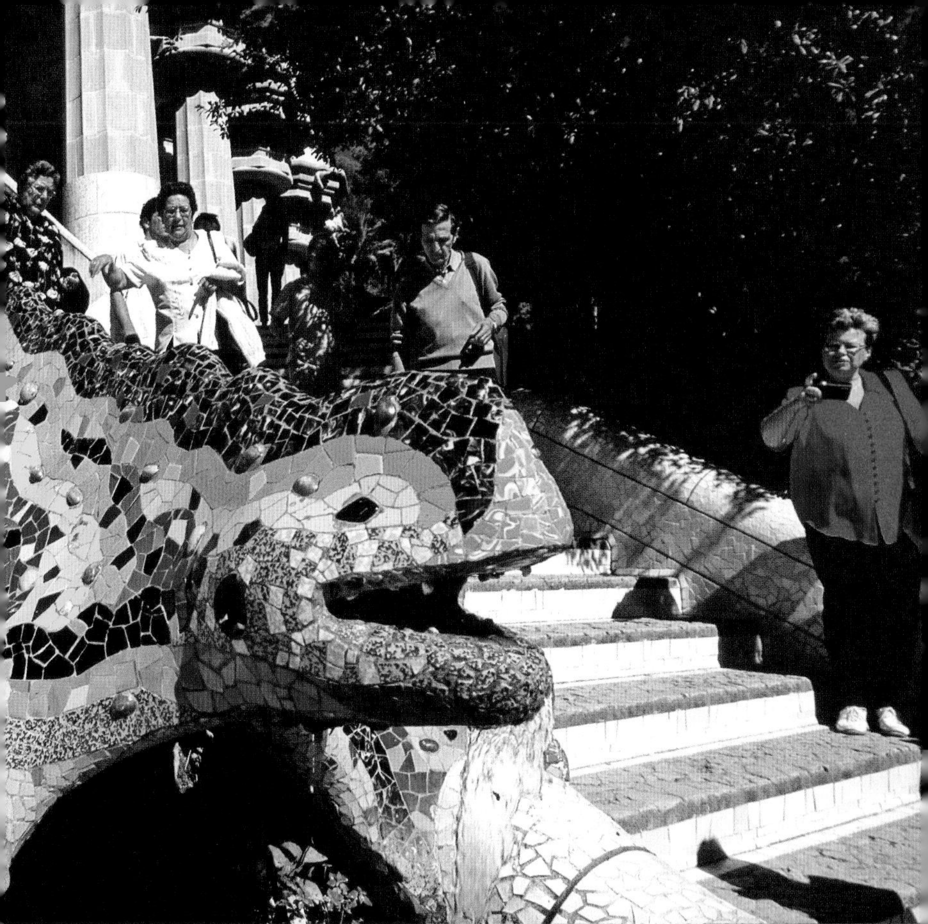

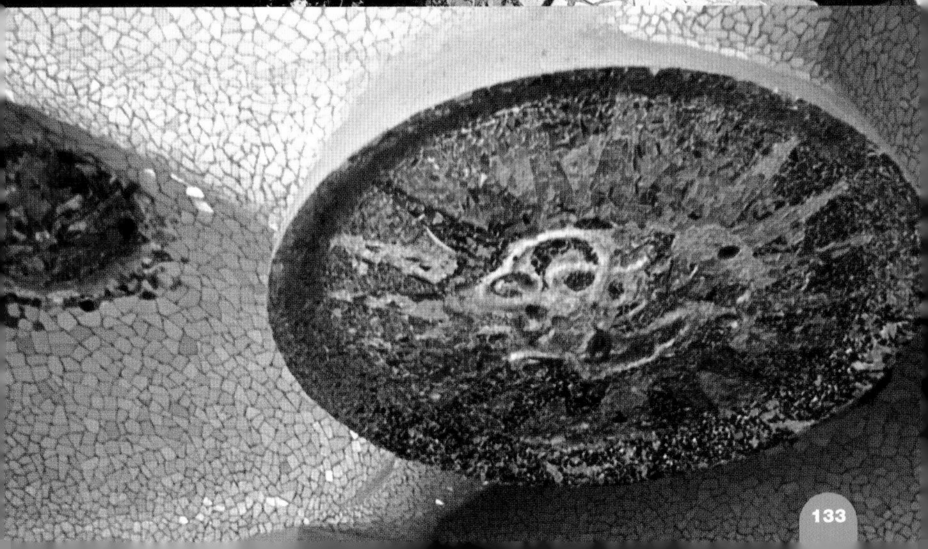

Parc del Laberint

Created by Italian architect Dominico Bagutti in the 18th century for the Desvalls family in the grounds of their grand estate, this is the oldest park in Barcelona and is a magnificent example of formal neoclassical parks of the era. It fell into disarray for many years, but was extensively refurbished in 1994.

This enchanting and romantic place is often overlooked by visitors as it's stuck a bit out of the way on top of a hill, in the outer suburb of Vall d'Hebron. However, it recently got an image boost as a location in the film *Perfume*, after which there has been an upsurge in the number of visitors.

The movie mostly featured the park's intricate and elegant maze, made from sculptured cypress trees, which leads to an elegant space with stone benches and a statue of Eros at the centre. The garden is arranged in Italianate style on various levels. Above the maze, a Love Canal winds

Above: The maze at Parc del Laberint

its way through ivy-clad banks and under balustraded bridges, ending at the Love Island. Originally, couples would have taken small boats along the canal, but now only swans take to the water. On the park's top level a neoclassical pavilion sits overlooking a large reflective pool. Throughout the park, paths wind through pine woods, sculptures, grottoes and fountains to create a fairy-tale atmosphere. The garden is intended as a living musuem, so there are strict rules banning dogs, bikes, roller skates and picnicking, in order to protect the peace and calm. But there is a bar, play area and picnic area located just outside the park's entrance.

✚ **113 C1**

✉ **Parc del Laberint**
Carrer del Germans Desvalls 1,
La Vall d'Hebron

☎ 93 428 3934

🕐 Daily 10am–dusk

✋ Inexpensive (free Sun and Wed), children under 5 free

🚇 Mundet

Sagrada Família

Gaudí's final unfinished masterpiece is a defining image of Barcelona, and no visit to the city would be complete without it. Its spires are visible from every vantage point over the city, and millions of tourists flock here every year.

The Templo Expiatorio de la Sagrada Família – its full title – was conceived by a bookseller, Josep Maria Bocabella, founder of an association dedicated to St Joseph. Inspired by the church of Loreto on a trip to Italy, Bocabella determined to create a similar building on his return.

In 1877, the association secured a plot of land in the new Eixample district, and accepted a neo-Gothic design by the architect Francesc de Paula del Villar. The first stone was laid in 1882, and Gaudí took over construction just one year later, at the age of 31, following conflict between Del Villar and the council over materials and budget. Overhauling del Villar's plans for his trademark Modernist style, he devoted the remainder of his life to the construction of the church. During his last years, funds for the construction were tight, but Gaudí became a fervent ambassador for the project, explaining it at great length to anyone who would listen, and even going into the street to ask for contributions from passers-by.

Left: The Sagrada Família, designed by Gaudí as "an immense palace of Christian memory"; **above right:** The spectacular interior of the church

✚ **113 C3**

✉ **Sagrada Família**
Carrer de Mallorca 401

☎ 93 207 3031

🌐 **www.sagradafamilia.org**

🕐 Apr–Sep, daily 9–8; Oct–Mar, 9–6

✋ Moderate (additional charge for life, inexpensive)

Ⓜ Sagrada Família

At the time of Gaudí's death in 1926 (he is now buried in the crypt of the church) only one façade, one tower, the apse and the crypt were finished. Few comprehensive plans were left behind, and many of those that did exist were destroyed by fire or in violence during the civil war, so the design now being worked on is based on reconstructions and modern interpretations.

A lack of funds and civil war slowed construction until the mid-1950s, and today, two façades and eight towers are complete. Currently, construction efforts are largely focused on the nave and the

Left: The footbridge linking two towers of the Nativity Façade; **above:** The church reflected in the placid waters in front

transept, including the hall of columns, the choir and high windows. When this is completed, the inside of the temple will be covered for the first time and building work will start on the central dome.

Work is expected to last until at least 2041. The final church will house 13,000 people, and have a total of 18 towers, representing the 12 Apostles, the 4 Evangelists, Jesus Christ and the Virgin Mary.

The church was intended to be the "last great sanctuary of Christendom" and the entire building is decorated in Christian allegory. The spectacular towers bear the legends "Hosanna", "Excelsis" and "Sanctus" and the doors to the Passion Façade reproduce words from the Bible in various languages.

The Passion Façade, on Carrer de Sardenya, is formed from sharp geometric shapes and is quite austere in style, with stark columns that resemble bones. The Nativity Façade on Carrer de la Marina features four spiny, spire-like bell towers and doors dedicated to the virtues Faith, Hope and Charity. The main façade of the building, the Glory Façade, has not yet been built. The 12 bell towers, which give the temple its very distinctive outline, represent the 12 Apostles. The initial

of each one is engraved on the top of each tower.

Initially, construction was expected to last for several hundred years, based on building techniques of the 1900s. However, computer technology has been used to speed things up, and much of the stone is now machined off-site. This is not without controversy, and it is felt by some that modern interpretations and materials detract a step too far from Gaudí's intent. A series of sculptures by Josep Subirachs of the crucified Christ were added in 1987, and these received much criticism for their style.

On April 22, 2007 a 3m (10-feet) high statue of Sant Jordi, the latest in the changing façade of the cathedral, was added.

There is an on-site museum where you can see stonemasons at work and see some pieces of ecclesiastical furniture designed by Gaudí for the temple, such as a confessional box. You can also visit the towers via a lift or a long climb up tight spiral staircases. It's very high and very narrow, so give it a miss if you are at all claustrophobic or suffer from vertigo.

Above: Intricately carved detail in the cloister; **right:** Carving on the Passion Façade

TIBERIVS

Further Afield

If time allows, it's worth heading into the outer reaches of the city, or out of town altogether, to gain a deeper understanding of Catalan life. Several of the city's most impressive, though perhaps less famous attractions, such as the Palau de Pedralbes, are situated on the outskirts, while the Parque de Collserolla offers great hiking less than 30 minutes from Plaça de Catalunya. Hop on a train and in less than an hour you can lose yourself in the lovely cobblestoned streets of the white-washed seaside town of Sitges, while another 30-minutes or so puts you in the heart of Tarragona – one of the most important Roman outposts on the Iberian peninsula.

Montserrat

The strange rounded fingers of the holy Montserrat mountain, just under an hour's drive northwest of Barcelona, can be seen for miles around, as it rises to 1,235m (4,052 feet).

It's an iconic, sacred mountain for the Catalans, who come here to kiss the hand of the Black Virgin (La Moreneta) – a 12th-century statue of the Virgin Mary, supposedly miraculously found in a cave on the mountain. She's now housed in a magnificent basilica. A special room is set aside for people to leave offerings, such as wedding dresses, photos, even cigarettes in the hope of, receiving a favour, such as having a baby, an illness being cured, or giving up smoking. The other big draw is the famous Montserrat boys choir, one of the oldest in Europe, which sings at services (Mon–Fri 1pm, Sun 12 noon and 6:45pm). The Montserrat monastery complex also has an art museum, featuring works by Picasso, El Greco and Monet.

The mountain used to be reachable by road or by rail and cable car only. This

vertiginous ride is now optional as there's a rack railway which takes a much slower and less hair-raising route to the mountain. Once on the mountain, funiculars take you to the start of hiking trails, such as the three-hour circular route to the Sant Jeroni lookout point (not for vertigo sufferers) with magnificent views. Information about other trails can be found at the Montserrat Tourist Office which, along with shops, restaurants, cafés and bars, is situated just below the Monastery complex, a short walk from the car park and railway/cable car drop-off points.

Above: The Montserrat Mountain, which encircles the red-roofed monastery

✉ **Montserrat**
Oficina de Turisme de Montserrat, Plaça de la Creu, Montserrat

☎ 093 877 7777

W
W
W **www.montserratvisita.com**

🕐 Jun–Sep, daily 9–8; Oct–May, 9–6

✋ Museum moderate

🚉 FGC Montserrat-Aeri (for cable car), Monistrol de Montserrat (for rack railway)

Museo Cau Ferrat

Cau Ferrat was the home and studio of Santiago Rusiñol, the leading name in the Catalan *Modernista* artworld. It's now a museum displaying his enormous collection of artworks – including works by himself and by friends and colleagues – and craftwork artefacts.

✉ **Museo Cau Ferrat**
   Carrer de Fonollar s/n,
   Sitges

☎ 93 894 0364

🌐 **www.diba.es/museus/
   sitges.asp**

🕑 Mid-Jun to Sep, Tue–Sat
   9:30–2, 4–7, Sun 10–3; Oct
   to mid-Jun, Tue–Sat 9:30–2,
   3:30–6:30, Sun 10–3

✋ Moderate (free first Wed of
   the month), children under
   12 free

🚊 RENFE Sitges

The building was made from converting and joining two fishermen's cottages. Architect Francesc Rogent turned these humble dwellings into a single neo-Gothic mini palace, using genuine Gothic windows that had been taken from Sitges' medieval castle. The high, airy rooms have exposed wooden beams, painted ceilings and warm colours that call to mind the earth and sea. They contain artworks by Rusiñol himself and fellow *Modernista* names such as Ramon Casas and Miquell Utrillo, as well as two works by El Greco. Rusiñol brought these pictures to Sitges in typically over-the-top style, carrying them through the streets at the head of a procession, complete with band. However, Rusiñol was a dedicated collector and the museum also displays his extensive collection of ceramics, glasswork and wrought-iron pieces.

Above: Holidaymakers relax in the waters and on the flat sandy beach, lined with palms and overlooked by cafés

Museu Maricel del Mar

The museum was originally built by American art collector Charles Deering, who wanted to emulate Rusiñol's Cau Ferrat, but the Palau Maricel fell into disuse when Deering returned home in 1921.

It reopened as an art museum in 1961 to house the treasures of another private collector, Dr Pérez Rosales. Like Cau Ferrat, the Maricel del Mar also has a fabulous *mirador* room overlooking the sea. If you tear yourself away from the view, you'll find a collection of Catalan sculpture in the same space. In the vestibule are allegorical works inspired by World War I, painted on silk in 1917 by Josep Maria Sert. Other exhibits include Romanesque murals, paintings on wood from the Gothic era, as well as altarpieces and religious

icons from the Renaissance period. Another section has work by Sitges-based artists from the Romantic period to the late 20th century. Other paintings depict traditional activities, such as fishing and picking the Malvasia grapes, painted by leading *Modernista* artists. Finally, the collection of Emerencià Roig consists of a wide range of artefacts from the marine world and includes interesting nautical instruments.

Above: The curvaceous statue of a mermaid that overlooks the water at Passeig Maritim

☒ **Museu Maricel del Mar**
Carrer de Fonollar s/n, Sitges

☎ 93 894 0364

🌐 **www.diba.es/museus/sitges.asp**

◉ Mid-Jun to Sep, Tue–Sat 9:30–2, 4–7, Sun 10–3; Oct to mid-Jun, Tue–Sat 9:30–2, 3:30–6:30, Sun 10–3

✋ Moderate (free first Wed of the month), children under 12 free

Ⓡ RENFE Sitges

Museu de la Ciencia – CosmoCaixa

This spectacular museum, at the foot of Tibidabo, has been lauded as the finest of its kind in Europe. Founded in 1980, the museum closed in 1998 for an overhaul that took six years to complete. It is now funded by the La Caixa Bank.

The original building, a poorhouse dating from the early 20th century, has been extended underground and renovated to create a high-tech interactive experience that dwarfs its predecessor. The permanent collection is divided into four sections – "Inert", "Living", "Intelligent" and "Civilized" Materials – moving from the Big Bang theory, through the first signs of life, the birth of mankind, human intelligence and the computer age. Multimedia installations bring the subject to life, and themed rooms include a living Amazon forest with over 100 species of animals and plants.

It's highly recommended for kids, with a multitude of hands-on activities, and animals including rats, frogs and spiders. You can experience an earthquake and hear whispers from a distance. There is also a geological wall, explaining the geological history of the world, and a planetarium.

✉ **Museu de la Ciencia**
Carrer de Teodor Roviralta 47-51

☎ 93 212 6050

🔳 **www.fundacio.lacaixa.es**

🕐 Tue–Sun 10–8

✋ Inexpensive (free first Sun of the month), children under 8 free

Ⓜ FGC Avenida Tibidabo

Left: Museu de la Ciencia housed in a splendid *Modernista* building; **below:** An exhibit outside the building

149

Museu–
Monestir de
Pedralbes

Founded in 1327 by the widowed
Queen Elisenda of Montcada, the
Monestir de Pedralbes still houses
a small closed order of Poor Clare
nuns, though most of this amazing
Gothic complex of church and
convent is now open to visitors.

Left: Intricate architectural details of
Monestrir de Pedralbes

The highlight is its beautiful cloister, with three floors of elegant arched arcades surrounding a green garden with palm trees, elegant cypresses and manicured lawns.

Visitors can get a glimpse of life in the medieval order by touring through the dormitory, vaulted refectory, chapterhouse, kitchens, pharmacy, abbey and day cells, and examining the display of everyday objects used by the nuns, from illuminated manuscripts to furniture. In the small chapel of Sant Miguel you'll find murals by a student of Giotto – local 14th-century painter Ferrer Bassa. The monastery museum used to house works of art from the Thyssen-Bornemisza collection, but these are now found in the MNAC museum on Montjuïc.

Above: The exterior of the Monestir de de Pedralbes

✉ **Museu–Monestir de Pedralbes**
Baixada del Monestir 9

☎ 93 203 9282

🌐 **www.museuhistoria.bcn.es**

🕐 Tue–Sun and hols 10–2

✋ Moderate (combined ticket for entry to Conjunt Monumental de la Plaça del Rei, Museu-Monestir de Pedralbes, Museu-Casa Verdaguer and Centre d'Interpretació i Acollida del Park Güell); children under 16 free (free first Sun of the month)

🚇 FGC Reina Elisenda

Nou Camp

The Nou Camp is the home of one of Europe's greatest football teams – FC Barcelona, with many trophies under its belts and many of the world's best players.

If you want to see a match at this football club (usually played Saturday or Sunday every other week), you'll either have to queue at the ticket office on the day of the game or pay over the odds through an agency. This 98,000-seat Nou Camp stadium has over 1,25,000 club members.

Alternatively, you can visit the stadium and the Nou Camp museum through a guided tour. This takes you through the tunnels to the pitch and the dugouts, to the visitors' changing rooms, and to the

president's box (where you're discouraged from playing with the replica European cup, which Barça won in 1992). The memorabilia on display in the museum concentrates on earlier glory years, when the likes of Maradona, Gary Lineker and Johan Cruyff put more than one in the back of the net.

Above: The interior of Nou Camp;
right: A Barca football club shirt

✉ **Nou Camp**
Avinguda Arístides Maillol s/n
(entrance gates 7 or 9)

☎ 902 189 900; 0034 93 496 3600
(from overseas only)

🌐 **www.fcbarcelona.com**

🕐 Non-match days Mon–Sat 10–6, Sun
10–2:30 (open until 8 Apr–Oct); last
tour one hour before closing).
Match days daily 10–3
(tour not available)

✋ Museum moerate; guided tour
(including museum) expensive,
children under 6 free

Ⓜ Collblanc or Palau Reial

Palau de Pedralbes

This royal palace was originally intended for the Güell family, Gaudí's patrons, but it was handed to King Alphonso XII for use during visits to the city. The luxurious grounds are now an elegant public park featuring mature trees, sculptures and fountains, including one designed by Gaudí himself.

The palace buildings now house the museums of ceramics and of decorative arts. The Museu de les Arts Decoratives opened in its present place and format in 1995, including for the first time an important collection of Spanish industrial design from the 1930s to the 1990s. The displays make a significant contribution to recounting the evolution of the decorative arts. The rest of the collection includes furniture from the Middle Ages to the present day including Renaissance and Gothic wedding chests; an array of glass goblets, jugs and other items, some of which date from the 6th century BC; jewellery, from exuberant Renaissance

and art nouveau jewels to avant garde contemporary designs. Also, there is a collection of pocket watches spanning three centuries; over a thousand pieces of historic wall coverings; and notable 19th-century carriages. Its sister institution, the Museu de Ceràmica houses an important collection of Spanish glazed ceramics from the 11th century to today and explores the substantial Spanish contribution to the craft. Some of the most interesting pieces are the ceramics produced by artists such as Picasso and Miró.

✉ **Palau de Pedralbes**
Palau Reial de Pedralbes, Avinguda Diagonal 686

☎ 93 280 5024

🌐 **www.museuartsdecoratives.es; www.museuceramica.bcn.es**

🕐 Tue–Sat 10–6, Sun 10–3

✋ Moderate, ticket admits to both museums (free first Sun of the month); grounds free

Ⓜ Palau Reial

Above: The decorated mansion house of the Palau de Pedralbes

Parc d'Atraccions de Tibidabo

The hill of Tibidabo looms over Barcelona, with its Christ-topped Sagrat Cor temple, a landmark visible from anywhere in the city. Getting here involves quite a trek, and the route is a combination of public transport: take the FGC to Av del Tibidabo, then the old-school tram Tramvia Blau to the foot of Tibidabo, from where a funicular railway takes you on the final hike.

At the top you'll find the Tibidabo funfair. Although it was first created in 1899, and features many historic rides and a museum of antique coin-operated fairground machines, it also has up-to-date, scream-inducing attractions, such as the first freefall ride in Spain, the Pendulum: a drop of 38m (124 feet) in 2.8 seconds. More gentle experiences include the pulse-raising log flume and the antique "flight simulator" – a slowly turning old-school biplane built in 1928. Other entertainment includes hourly puppet shows at the Marionetàrium and firework parades in the summer.

Below: The park features traditional fairground rides

Far left: The amusement park built on layers of mountain top

✉ **Parc d'Atraccions de Tibidabo**
Pl del Tibidabo 3–4

☎ 93 211 7942

🖥 **www.tibidado.es**

🕐 Mar–Jun and Sep–Dec, Sat–Sun and public holidays noon–6 or 10pm; Jul–Aug, Wed–Sun noon–10 or 11pm; first few days after Jan 1 11–4 or 5pm

✋ Expensive; children under 90cm and adults over 60 not going on attractons or attending shows free

🚇 FGC Av del Tibidabo

Tarragona

Today Tarragona is rather overshadowed, especially in tourism terms, by Barcelona. But a couple of millennia ago, the positions were reversed. Tarragona was the first Roman city to be built outside Italy, and it was such a big and bustling centre of commerce and government that remains pop up everywhere in modern-day Tarragona: the local Eroski supermarket has a Roman necropolis in its underground car park.

A good place to start a tour of Roman Tarragona is the Portal del Roser (Avinguda Catalunya), the entrance to the Passeig Arqueològic, a kilometre (0.5 mile) route along the path of the old Roman and medieval walls. The former Roman Praetorium (Tel: 97 724 1952) is rumoured to be the birthplace of Pontius Pilate. Near by, the circus was, in its heyday, one of the biggest in the empire, with space

for 30,000 spectators. One of the most impressive Roman sights is another place of entertainment, the Roman ampitheatre, Parc del Miracle (Tel: 97 724 2579), where up to 14,000 people would gather for such spectacles as chariot races and executions. One of the executions witnessed was that of St Fructuos. You can see the remains of a church dedicated to his memory, built when the amphitheatre became a Christian

temple in the 7th century AD. Near by, a more modern meeting place is the Balcó del Mediterrani, where locals always pass on their daily *paseo*. It's traditional to touch the iron railings for good luck. The Balcó has great views of the amphitheatre and the sea. Back in the upper part of town, the Catedral de Santa Maria is the largest in Catalunya. Built on the site of a Roman temple to Jupiter in the 12th century, its star attractions are its rose window and eye-grabbing portal, with statues of the 12 Apostles and the Madonna, as well as an attractive cloister. On Sunday mornings an antiques market is held close by.

To see some of the more interesting sights of modern-day Tarragona, take a stroll through the Serallo fishermen's districts where small boats still bring in their haul in the late afternoon. For fish-lovers some of the best restaurants are here, too. To relax after all the sightseeing, take a towel down to one of Tarragona's city beaches, such as the the Platja Llarga or the Platja de la Rabassada. It's the perfect way to unwind.

Above left: A street in the Roman town of Tarragona ; **above right:** The large cloistered garden courtyard of Tarragona's cathedral

✉ **Tarragona**
Oficina de Turisme de Tarragona, Carrer Major 39, Tarragona

☎ 97 725 0795

🌐 **www.tarragonaturisme.es**

🚉 RENFE Tarragona

Listings

Barcelona is a city of culture in every sense of the word. From Gaudí's eye-popping architecture to the city's Gothic heart, the ports and the shoreline, and the rippling spine of the Collserola mountains and Montjuïc which are home to several important museums and formal gardens, it has more than enough to keep culture vultures coming back for years. For art-lovers the city represents some of the 20th century's greatest painters, including Picasso and Joan Miró, while design and architecture buffs will delight in the modern architecture that is making its mark on the cityscape of the 21st century. Perhaps the best way to appreciate the "great seductress" is not so much by visiting the art galleries and museums, but by roaming the streets and simply watching the world go by in the outdoor cafés and restaurants.

Accommodation

Barcelona offers some of the most varied accommodation options in Europe. From state-of-the-art business hotels to colourful B&Bs, swish designer 5-star hotels to boutique town houses, the city now has something to suit every budget (with increasingly attractive options in the mid-range market). The excellent public transport systesm makes all areas of the city easily accessible. What you do need to know is that with the Catalan capital's increased popularity, peak time is now all year round and availability can be a problem, so book as far in advance as possible to avoid disappointment. Also keep in mind that rates can go up considerably during trade fairs.

€ under 100
€€ 100–200
€€€ 200–300
€€€€ over 300

MONTJUÏC & RAVAL

AC Miramar €€€
Perched on Montjuïc Mountain, the AC chain's flagship hotel offers impressive views and deluxe leisure features, such as a fibre-optic-lit swimming pool and spa facilities. The rooms are spacious, some with private terraces and hot tubs.
✉ Plaça Carlos Ibáñez 3, Passeig de Miramar, Montjuïc ☎ 93 281 1600 ⓦ www.ac-hotels.com ⓠ Funicular de Montjuïc

Casa Camper €€
Casa Camper occupies a prime spot in trendy El Raval, just around the corner from the MACBA. It's minimalist and edgy with a serve-yourself kitchen supplying free snacks and drinks instead of room service. Each comfortably appointed room comes with its own private living room, where you'll find a flat-screen TV and a hammock.
✉ Carrer d'Elisabets 11 ☎ 93 342 6280 ⓦ www.casacamper.com ⓠ Catalunya

Chic & Basic Tallers €

This ultra-chic hostel sets a new standard in budget accommodation. The slick, functional rooms are equipped with an MP3 system and a flat-screen TV while in the retro bar area downstairs you can make a cup of tea or coffee.

✉ Carrer dels Tallers 82 ☎ 93 302 5183 ⊠ www.chicandbasic.com ⓠ Universitat, Catalunya

Eurostars Grand Marina €€€€

Almost a private island, this 5-star hotel is within the World Trade Centre on a piece of land jutting into Barcelona's commercial harbour. The spacious, minimalist interior can feel a bit soulless, though there are attempts to bring some life to the place with entertainment options such as Opera Saturdays, live music evenings and a gourmet restaurant specialising in cuisine from the North of Spain.

✉ World Trade Centre, Moll de Barcelona s/n ☎ 93 603 9000 ⊠ www.granmarinahotel.com ⓠ Drassanes

Gat Xino €

Gat Xino offers true boutique-style accommodation at prices that wouldn't break the bank. Sleek interiors with acid green accents, free internet access, retro designer furniture and the odd original artwork, plus a sunny roof terrace and wood-decked breakfast room match the colourful personality of this place.

✉ Carrer de l'Hospital 149–155 ☎ 93 324 8833 ⊠ www.gataccomodation.com ⓠ Liceu

Market Hotel €

A newcomer that's received rave reviews since opening, this stylish town-house is located in the quiet, leafy neighbourhood of Sant Antoni. Rooms are spacious with dark wood floors and lacquered oriental furniture, and luxurious black bathrooms.

✉ Carrer de Compte Borrell 68

☎ 93 325 1205 ⊠ www.markethotel.com.es ⓠ Sant Antoni, Urgell

LAS RAMBLAS & BARRI GÒTIC

Bonic B&B €

This cute urban guesthouse has just eight colourfully decorated rooms with Spanish-Moorish flourishes. They share three clean, comfortable bathrooms. The friendly owners have added lots of little extras ensuring guests feel that this is their home-away-from-home, including complimentary tea, coffee, pastries and water, plentiful newspapers and magazines, and free internet access.

✉ Carrer de Josep Anselm Clavé 9 10–4ª ☎ 626 053 434 ⊠ www.bonic-barcelona. com ⓠ Drassanes, Barceloneta

Duquesa de Cardona €€€

A charming, romantic hotel facing the Port Vell, it remains surprisingly undiscovered, which is part of its charm. The dining room boasts graceful, soaring arches while the roof terrace provides a more casual space for evening cocktails, bistro-style food and splashing around in the pool. The rooms are on the small side and its worth going for the deluxe option if you need more space.

✉ Passeig de Colom 12 ☎ 93 268 9090 ⊠ www.hduquesadecardona.com ⓠ Drassanes

H10 Racó del Pi €€

For many it's the best location in the city: a prime spot overlooking lovely Plaça del Pi with its lively bars and art market bustle putting you right in the heart of the action. It's also not a bad little hotel with clean, comfortable rooms (all with free internet access), helpful staff, a decent breakfast and a complimentary glass of *cava* on arrival. Note that the surrounding area can get noisy at night.

✉ Carrer del Pi 7 ☎ 93 342 6190 ⊠ www.hotelracodelpi.com ⓠ Liceu

H1898 €€€

While the Ramblas can be noisy and many of its grand hotels have seen better days, the H1898 offers a touch of class. Located in the old 1881 Philippine Tobacco Company building, its imposing walls ooze history contrasted by its interior candy striped walls. The roof terrace is huge, and the plush Roman-style spa in the basement offers a range of pampering treatments. Suites on the Ramblas have private, exterior plunge pools.

✉ La Rambla 109 (entrance on Carrer delPintor Fortuny) ☎ 93 552 9552 🖳 www.nnhotels.com 🚇 Catalunya

Hotel Neri €€€€

One of the most romantic hotels in the city, this 18th-century palace has been revamped up with plush red velvet sofas and silk bed spreads effectively creating a magical retreat from the bustle of the old quarter. A gourmet restaurant, lushly planted roof terrace, and the occasional celebrity guest all add to the glam factor.

✉ Carrer de Sant Sever 5 ☎ 93 304 0655 🖳 www.hotelneri.com 🚇 Jaume I

PORT VELL & LA RIBERA

Arts €€€€

This is where visiting A-listers stay when they're in town for the unsurpassed service and impressive facilities including James Bond style duplex suites. The skyscraper on the beach has two world-class restaurants, a 43rd-floor spa and a swimming pool set in gardens dotted with hammocks.

✉ Carrer de la Marina 19–21 ☎ 93 221 1000 🖳 www.hotelartsbarcelona.com 🚇 Ciutadella-Port Olímpic

Banys Orientals €

This designer hotel occupies a smart town-house in the heart of the Born. Its soft lighting, high-quality linens and designer touches more than make up for the slightly small rooms. It also has a great location in terms of bars, restaurants and cafés.

✉ Carrer de l'Argenteria 37 ☎ 93 268 8460 🖳 www.hotelbanysorientals.com 🚇 Jaume I

Chic & Basic Hotel €€

Its white-on-white colour scheme is almost blinding, but it's great for fashionistas on a budget. Rooms come with nice touches such as the mirrored cornices for reflecting original features you might not otherwise see. It also has a handy communal lounge with free tea, coffee and snacks on tap. The White Bar downstairs has a popular DJ spot on Friday nights.

✉ Carrer de la Princesa 50 ☎ 93 295 4652 🖳 www.chicandbasic.com 🚇 Jaume I

Grand Hotel Central €€€

Lauded for its fantastic roof-top swimming pool, the rest of the hotel isn't quite so breathtaking. Rooms are self-consciously minimal with black accents, and the lighting can be frustratingly dim. Staff, however, are friendly and helpful, and the trendy bar and restaurant in the basement is good for making new friends.

✉ Vía Laietana 30 ☎ 93 295 7900 🖳 www.grandhotelcentral.com 🚇 Jaume I

Hotel Ciutat Barcelona €€

In the middle of the Born, this simple hotel is all about no frills, no fuss. The rooms are small, simple and functional with pocket-sized bathrooms. Where it scores, though, is in its location and its wonderful roof terrace with plunge pool, wet bar and views over neighbouring rooftops.

✉ Carrer de la Princesa 33 ☎ 93 269 7475 🖳 www.ciutatbarcelona.com 🚇 Jaume I

Hotel 54 Barceloneta €€

This newly opened boutique hotel near the beach in Barceloneta, with fantastic views over the yachts in the Port Vell, is already in hot demand. The rooms are fun and funky with mood-colour lighting, and the roof terrace is a blissful spot to watch the sun go down.

✉ Passeig Joan de Borbó 54 ☎ 93 225 0054 ⓦ www.hotel54barceloneta.com
Ⓜ Barceloneta

L'EIXAMPLE

Granados 83 €€

With decor that wouldn't look out of place in New York's Tribeca neighbourhood, this stylish boutique hotel has a retro cocktail bar, a rooftop terrace and pool, and a gourmet restaurant.

✉ Carrer d'Enric Granados 83
☎ 93 492 9670 ⓦ www.derbyhotels.com
Ⓜ Universitat

Hesperia Tower €€€

Located between the city and the airport, this is the hotel of the moment for discerning business travellers. Designed by Richard Rogers, the monolithic, red scaffold-clad structure affords impressive views of the world below. Rooms are sumptuous with floor-to-ceiling windows and large bathrooms. A wine bar, the city's biggest wellness centre and a dramatic penthouse restaurant headed by Michelin-starred Santi Santamaria make it a memorable stopover. It has some excellent deals online.

✉ Gran Via 144, L'Hospitalet de llobregat
☎ 93 413 5000 ⓦ www.hesperia-tower.com
Ⓜ Hospital de Bellvitge

Hotel Prestige Paseo de Gràcia €€€

Business orientated with designer touches, the Prestige is perfectly located for shopaholics. With its hip library and WiFi zones, elegant bedrooms and unique "Ask Me" service that allows visitors to tap into insider knowledge about the city, it's a good choice for travellers looking for a DIY tailor-made experience.

✉ Passeig de Gràcia 62 ☎ 93 272 4180
ⓦ www.prestigepaseodegracia.com
Ⓜ Passeig de Gràcia, Diagonal

Omm €€€

This award-winning, contemporary hotel is convenient for designer stores and high-street flagship shops on Passeig de Gràcia and Diagonal. Rooms are sleekly minimal without being austere, with twin-sink bathrooms. Other 5-star features include a Michelin starred restaurant, Moo; trendy nightclub soundproofed in the basement; deluxe spa, and rooftop plunge pool with views over Gaudí's *Witch Scarers* at nearby La Pedrera.

✉ Carrer del Rosselló 265 ☎ 93 445 4000
ⓦ www.hotelomm.es
Ⓜ Diagonal, Passeig de Gràcia

Pulitzer €€€

This smart, centrally located hotel deserves far more attention than it gets. The vast lobby lounge filled with fat, white leather sofas and contemporary art-works is a hot spot for Sunday morning Bloody Mary's and pre-dinner cocktails. The roof terrace is lushly planted and hosts Thursday night parties, and the bedrooms have an edgy, designer. Check out special deals such as the celebration breakfast in bed complete with roses and champagne followed by a foam bath.

✉ Carrer de Bergara 8 ☎ 93 481 6767
ⓦ www.hotelpulitzer.es Ⓜ Catalunya

SoHo €€

The NN group has broken new ground with its boutique chain concept with several new openings around town. The SoHo was designed by local architect Alfredo Arribas with a crystal art-work in the reception that is reflected throughout. Seventh-floor rooms are the best, with large terraces, while the rooftop has a plunge pool and wet bar. There's a wood-decked terrace off the breakfast room, and although there's no formal restaurant it does have 24-hour room service.

✉ Gran Via 543–545
☎ 93 552 9610 ⓦ www.nnhotels.com
Ⓜ Urgell

Restaurants

With the rise of superstar chefs like Ferran Adrià taking the world by storm, Barcelona is now one of the world's leading destinations for food-lovers. In the space of a weekend, visitors can explore a multitude of possibilities from feasting on market-fresh produce in the Boqueria food market, to stimulating the senses with exciting, new-wave Spanish cuisine. You can have a traditional paella lunch on the beach or join locals in the convivial art of the *tapeo* (tapas crawl). Whatever your penchant, there's something for everyone in Catalonia's gastronomic capital.

€ upto €20
€€ €20–35
€€€ €30 or above

MONTJUÏC & RAVAL

Bar Lobo €

The newest of the Tragaluz Group's ever-growing empire, this trendy bar-cum-restaurant is their first venture into the old town and brings a bright dose of uptown panache with it. It's great for light fare such as fresh salads and pasta dishes, as well as tasty vegetarian options.
⊠ Carrer de Pintor Fortuny 2 ☎ 93 481 5346
🕓 Daily 1:30–4, 8:30–11 🅠 Liceu

El Jardí €

This charming courtyard within the former Antic Hospital de la Santa Creu & La Capella (now Barcelona's main library) is a lovely place for a long, lazy lunch. The kitchen takes two fresh daily deliveries from the Boqueria and turns them into pan-Mediterranean dishes. By night part of it becomes a chilled-out wine bar complete with cushions and candles.
⊠ Carrer de l'Hospital 56 ☎ 93 329 1550
🕓 Mon–Sat 10am–midnight 🅠 Liceu

Inopia €€

This lively tapas bar is co-owned by Albert Adrià (the pastry chef at El Bulli, named one of the world's greatest restaurants) and his childhood friend Joan Martínez. Don't expect anything crazy here though – this is traditional tapas at its best, served in a busy and bright environment.

✉ C/Tamarit 104 ☎ 93 424 5231
🆆 www.barinopia.com 🕐 Tue–Fri 7–11, Sat 1–3:30, 7–11 Ⓜ Poble Sec

La Bella Napoli €

Great pizza is tough to find in Barcelona, so it's worth heading away from the city centre for this genuine family-run Neapolitan trattoria. Choose from excellent home-made mozzarella and *arrocine* (rice balls), and perfectly thin, crisp pizza bases with extravagant toppings such as Sophia Loren's *rucola* and parmesan pie.

✉ Carrer de Margarit 14 ☎ 93 442 5056
🕐 Tue–Sun 1:30–4, 8:30–midnight
Ⓜ Paral.lel

Mam i Teca €€

This pint-sized corner bar is a gem, with bright yellow walls, green trim, a massive chandelier and a wall filled with enough exotic alcohol to make any cocktail bar proud. Its relaxed atmosphere, interesting Spanish wine list and top-notch, locally sourced ingredients have brought it cult status. The succulent lamb chops are superb, as are the peppery *botifarras* (Catalan sausages).

✉ Carrer de la Lluna 4 ☎ 93 441 3335
🕐 Mon, Wed–Fri and Sun 1pm–midnight, Sat 8:30pm–midnight Ⓜ Sant Antoni

Quimet I Quimet €€

A Barcelona classic that attracts foodies from all over the world who come to sample Quim's legendary *montaditos* (small mounted sandwiches) with toppings such as coarse pork pate with onion jam; prawns, caviar and honey; and creamy goat's cheese with candied chestnuts. Lined floor to ceiling with wine bottles, with space for only three high tables, it's the perfect place to kick-start your evening.

✉ Carrer del Poeta Cabanyes 25 ☎ 93 442 3142 🕐 Mon–Fri noon–4, 7:30–10:30, Sat noon–4 Ⓜ Paral.lel

Rias de Galicia €€€

A favourite among Catalonia's top chefs for delicious seafood, Rias de Galicia is one of the few restaurants in the city that offers all the maritime wonders of the Boqueria food market. Feast on heap platters of *percebes* (goose barnacles), sea snails and *erizos de mar* (sea urchins) and wash it down with delectable, ozone-fresh *albariño* wine from Galicia.

✉ Carrer de Lleida 7 ☎ 93 424 8152
🆆 www.riasdegalicia.com 🕐 Tue–Sat 1:30–4, 8:30–11 Ⓜ Plaça de Espanya, Poble Sec

Rosal 34 €€€

A newcomer to Barcelona's ever-growing circuit of high-end, modern tapas bars, this smart New York loft-style space has a laid-back feel, friendly service and classy cuisine. Dishes change seasonally but include such delights as artichoke hearts stuffed with a soft-poached quail's egg topped with caviar, and foie gras with candied lemon.

✉ Carrer del Roser 34 ☎ 93 324 9046
🆆 www.rosal34.com
🕐 Mon 8:30pm–11:30pm, Tue–Sat 1:30–4, 8:30–11:30 Ⓜ Paral.lel

Sésamo €

While most of the vegetarian offerings in Barcelona are still fairly mundane, Sésamo is a member of the Slow Food movement and offers lively, imaginative dishes in an upbeat, trendy environment. Situated right next to the Sant Antoni market, freshness is guaranteed, with such delightful dishes as fennel carpaccio with olives and oranges, and *gyozo* dumplings stuffed with creamy Catalan cheese.

✉ Carrer de Sant Antoni Abat 52
☎ 93 441 6411 🆆 www.sesamo-bcn.com
🕐 Mon and Wed–Sat 1–5, 8–1, Sun 8pm–1am Ⓜ Sant Antoni

Tapioles 53 €€

An informal, secret dining room in deepest, darkest Poble Sec, where Australian chef Sarah Stothart dishes up whatever she fancies to hordes of "gastroclub" fans from all over the world. Sourcing her ingredients from three of the city's markets, she cooks according to old family favourites, changing the menu every week. The small but perfectly formed menu of two starters, two mains and dessert includes dishes such as *osso bucco* and gorgonzola-and-pear-stuffed ravioli. Reservations essential.

✉ C/Tapioles 53 ☎ 93 329 2238 www.tapioles53.com ⏰ Tue–Sat 8:30–midnight ⓜ Paral.lel, Poble Sec

LAS RAMBLAS & BARRI GÒTIC

Cafè de l'Academia €€

Classic Catalan cooking with a twist is the order of the day at this popular bistro. The red-brick interior and candlelight give it an intimate ambience, while tables on the terrace are some of the most coveted in the city. Try the salt cod with artichokes, roast guinea fowl with apple tart, and silky Catalan custard, *crema catalana*.

✉ Carrer de Lledó 1 ☎ 93 319 8253 ⏰ Mon–Fri 9–4, 8:45–11:30 ⓜ Jaume I

Can Culleretes €

The oldest restaurant in Barcelona is as busy today as it was when it first started doing business in 1786, and dining here is part of the Barcelona pilgrimage. Book ahead to get a table in one of its several, old-school dining rooms to enjoy Catalan classics such as roast goose and pears.

✉ C/Quintana 5 ☎ 93 317 3022 www.culleretes.com ⏰ Tue–Sat 1:30–4, 9–11, Sun 1:30–4 ⓜ Liceu

Cerveceria Taller de Tapas €

Inspired by the specialties of different regions of Spain, Taller de Tapas offers around 50 freshly made tapas, including chorizos in cider from Galicia, fresh spinach with raisins and pine nuts, and lip-smacking Palamos prawns from the Costa Brava. The latest addition to the Taller family is a *cervecería* (beer house) opened early in 2007, which adds satisfying plates of Spanish soul food like *pollo al ajillo* (chicken stewed in garlic) and juicy home-made burgers to its repertoire.

✉ Carrer de Comtal 28 ☎ 93 481 6233 www.tallerdetapas.com ⏰ Mon–Fri 9am–midnight, Sat–Sun 9am–1am ⓜ Urquinaona

Els Quatre Gats €€

This is where the painter Pablo Picasso got his first break: designing the menu. Relics of his works and other artworks of the era decorate the walls, while a pianist serenades diners. If romance is on the agenda, book a table for two on the mezzanine which gives a bird's-eye view of the surroundings. The food is unlikely to win any Michelin stars, but the salt-baked fish and slow-roast lamb are both reliable.

✉ Carrer de Montsió 3 ☎ 93 302 4140 www.4gats.com ⏰ Mon–Sun 8am–1am ⓜ Urquinaona, Catalunya

Kiosko Universal €€

Situated in the bustle of the market with a long bar and several high tables under the arches of the Boqueria, the Kiosko Universal serves fresh fish and seafood straight from the neighbouring stalls. Arrive before 1.30pm to avoid waiting.

✉ Mercat de la Boqueria ⏰ Mon–Sat 9–4 ⓜ Liceu

Kyonoto €€

This fashionable sushi place incorporates all the elements of a cool night out: lounge music, sake cocktails and fantastic sushi and sashimi. The loft-style interior and floor-to-ceiling windows suggest New York's Meatpacking district, but the laid-back ambience and affordable prices are 100 per cent Barcelona.

✉ Carrer de la Ciutat 5 ☎ 93 304 2376

🌐 www.kynoto.com 🕐 Mon–Fri noon–2am, Sat–Sun 8:30pm–2am 🚇 Jaume I

La Plata €

Old-fashioned tiles on the walls, barrels of lusty local wine, and sawdust on the floor set the mood at this superb tapas bar. The menu consists of fresh fried fish, grilled sausages on tasty bread and a dazzling tomato salad with or without anchovies.

✉ Carrer de la Merce 28 ☎ 93 315 1009 🕐 Tue–Sat 10–4, 7–10pm 🚇 Drassanes

Shunka €€€

When Catalonia's celebrity chefs Ferran Adrià and Santi Santamaria want Japanese food they head straight for Shunka. This place serves top-class sushi and noodle dishes in a clandestine dining room near the cathedral. Reserve a place at the bar to see the thrilling "dances of knives".

✉ C/Sagristans 5 ☎ 93 412 4991 🕐 Tue–Fri 1:30–3:30, 8:30–11:30, Sat–Sun 2–4, 8:30–11:30 🚇 Urquinaona, Catalunya

PORT VELL & LA RIBERA

7 Portes €€€

If it's good enough for Winston Churchill and Che Guevara, then it's good enough for the rest of us. 7 Portes is a Barcelona institution. The marble floors, bright orange lampshades and bow-tied waiters make it an experience in more ways than one. Do try the extensive range of paellas.

✉ Passeig d'Isabel II 14 ☎ 93 319 2950 🌐 www.7portes.com 🕐 Mon–Sun 1pm–1am 🚇 Barceloneta

Cava Mar €€

A trendy newcomer to Barceloneta with a gorgeous sea-facing terrace. Cava Mar lends a touch of fun to the typical menus of the *barrio,* such as gazpacho with watermelon and creamy shrimp and pea risotto. It's also a great spot for a glass of bubbly by the sea.

✉ Carrer Vila Joiosa 52 ☎ 93 225 7164 🌐 www.cavamar.com 🕐 Sun–Thu 11–8, Fri–Sat 11–2 🚇 Barceloneta

De Mercat (Barceloneta market) €€

The sleek backdrop of white on white and giant picture windows of this newly opened restaurant lend a more upscale mood to Barceloneta's spanking new market, a sign of things to come as the area gets increasingly gentrified and ever-more popular with tourists. Expect modern interpretation's of old fishing-village classics such as *fideus,* paella and seafood.

✉ Mercat de la Barceloneta s/n, Plaça de la Font 1 ☎ 93 221 6471 🕐 Mon–Sat 8am–midnight, Sun 8–4 🚇 Barceloneta

El Passadís del Pep €€€

El Passadís del Pep is a semi-private dining room where the chef does the ordering for you and the menu consists of locally sourced, fresh fish and seafood. Hidden down an alleyway, its secluded location, together with the white linen and the finely-dressed waiters give it the feel of a very posh restaurant.

✉ Plaça del Palau 2 ☎ 93 310 1021 🌐 www.passadis.com 🕐 Mon 9pm–11:30pm, Tue–Sat 1:30–4, 9–11:30 🚇 Barceloneta

Kaiku €€

Such is the popularity of this beachside restaurant that booking well in advance has become essential. Chef Hugo Pla i Cortès makes the best paella in Barceloneta, using interesting ingredients such as smoked rice, wild mushrooms and artichokes, as well as more traditional recipes.

✉ Passeig Joan de Borbó 74 ☎ 93 221 9082 🕐 Tue–Sun 1:30–4 🚇 Barceloneta

La Taberna de'n Pep €€

A great little hideaway, this cosy eatery used to be a *charcuteria* and butcher's shop. You can still stock up on *jamón* and sausages here, but it's also a fun place for lunch on a blustery day offering a hearty, meaty menu of classics like sausage and beans, roast artichokes with *romesco* sauce and rich casseroles.

✉ **Carrer de Sant Miquel 23** ☎ 93 221 8912
🕐 Mon–Fri 9–4, 7–11, Sat 9–4
🚇 Barceloneta, Jaume I

Mondo €€€

The swankiest new restaurant in the Port Vell serves upmarket fish dishes and perfectly cooked Galician seafood in a clubby, upbeat atmosphere. The red-and-white interior, harbour views, terrace, and add-on nightclub make it one of the city's coolest destinations.

✉ **Imax Building, Moll d'Espanya, Maremàgnum** ☎ 93 221 3911
🌐 www.mondobcn.com
🕐 Wed–Sun 1–4, 8–11pm) 🚇 Drassanes, Barceloneta

Mosquito €

A tapas bar with an Asian twist, Mosquito offers snack-sized portions of dishes from all over Asia, from Indian potato *chaat* to pork and rice noodle cakes. It also offers a good Japanese lunchtime menu. Lively and fun, Mosquito is a favourite with the local crowd.

✉ **Carrer dels Carders 46** ☎ 93 268 7569
🌐 www.mosquitotapas.com
🕐 Tue–Thu and Sun 1–1, Fri–Sat 1pm–3am
🚇 Arc de Triomf, Jaume I

Senyor Parellada €€

One of the prettiest and most reliable places in the city for sampling authentic Catalan cooking such as roast lamb with 12 heads of garlic, as well as excellent daily specials. The attractive dining room is arranged around a split-level courtyard and a touch of glitz is added by the lovely hanging chandeliers.

✉ **Carrer de Argenteria 3** ☎ 93 310 5094
🌐 www.senyorparellada.com
🕐 Daily 1–4, 8:30–midnight 🚇 Jaume I

Torre de Altamar €€€

One of the most expensive restaurants in Barelona, the "tower high above the sea" perches above the harbour and offers incredible views of the city. The modern Mediterranean menu is usually good, but occasionally falters.

✉ **Passeig Joan de Borbó 88**
☎ 93 221 0007 🌐 www.torredealtamar.com
🕐 Mon–Sat 1–3:30, 7–11:30
🚇 Barceloneta

Wushu €

Tiny Wushu offers superb, home-made dishes from all over Asia, such as Vietnamese salad rolls, Malaysian *laksa* and Thai curries. Daily specials are always interesting, while the desserts may well be among the best in town. Welcoming service and a lively atmosphere provide the icing on the cake.

✉ **Carrer de Colomines 2** ☎ 93 310 7313
🕐 Noon–midnight 🚇 Arc de Triomf, Jaume I

L'EIXAMPLE

Caelis €€€

The Michelin-starred Caelis at the Hotel Palace is a must for serious gourmands, offering modern Mediterranean dishes such as asparagus custard, market-fresh fish with lemon purée, and foie gras complemented by smoky slivers of eel. It has a smart, minimalist dining room and comes top of its class for style and service.

✉ **Gran Via de les Corts Catalanes 668**
☎ 93 510 1205 🌐 www.caelis.com
🕐 Tue–Fri 1:30–3:30, 8:30–11, Sat 8:30pm–11pm 🚇 Urquinaoa

Cinc Sentits €€€

A favourite among local and visiting foodies, Chef Jordi Artal's exciting interpretations of Catalan cuisine never fail to delight. The local seasonal menu is hot on new techniques and flavours, and it's worth opting for the "Omakase" (chef's surprise) menu for the wow factor.

✉ Carrer d'Aribau 58 ☎ 93 323 9490
🌐 www.cincsentits.com 🕐 Mon 1:30–3:30,
Tue–Sat 1:30–3:30, 8:30–11 Ⓜ Universitat

Niu Toc €€

This casual bistro on a pretty, quiet *plaça*
is a great place for sampling *bacalao* (salt
cod). With charming service and a good
range of fresh fish, it's perfect for a long
lazy lunch in the sun.
✉ Plaça de la Revolució de Setembre de
1868 ☎ 93 213 7461 🕐 Tue–Sat 1:30–4,
9–11, Sun 1:30–4pm Ⓜ Joanic, FCG Gràcia

Oli en un LLum €€

A clandestine cocktail bar with a smart
sandwich-cum-tapas bar beneath, this is
a good option for classy late-night snacks.
Don't miss the special here – a glass of
filomena (a heady blend of light Spanish
beer and stout), and truly sumptuous fried
egg and Iberian *jamón* sandwiches: a lip-
smacking combination.
✉ Passatge Bon Pastor 6 bis
☎ 93 201 7397 🌐 www.luzdegas.com
🕐 Daily 7:30pm–2am Ⓜ FCG Provença

Paco Meralgo €€

Paco Meralgo is a modern, bustling tapas
bar done up in cream and blonde wood
with slate-grey accents. Friendly waiters,
a distinctive uptown buzz and top-quality
Spanish charcuterie and seafood make it a
place to linger.
✉ Carrer de Muntaner 171 ☎ 93 430 9027
🌐 www.pacomeralgo.com
🕐 Daily 1–4, 8pm–12:30
Ⓜ Hospital Clínic, FCG Provença

Saüc €€€

A fine example of the extraordinary talent
of Catalonia's young chefs, this intimate
restaurant is headed by Xavier Franco who
earned his stripes at several of the city's
top eateries. His dishes include unusual
ingredients like tuna belly with blackcurrant
custard, and duck liver with cherry chutney
and orange blossom.

✉ Passatge. Lluís Pellicer 12 ☎ 93 321
0189 🌐 www.saucrestaurant.com
🕐 Tue–Sat 1:30–3:30, 8:30–10:30
Ⓜ Hospital Clínic

Shibui €€€

This is one of Barcelona's premier
Japanese restaurants offering superlative
sushi and teppanyaki dishes in a basement
dining room.
✉ Carrer de Comte d'Urgell 272–274 ☎ 93
321 9004 🌐 www.shibuirestaurantes.com
🕐 Mon–Sat 1–3:30, 8:30–11:30
Ⓜ Hospital Clínic

Speakeasy €€€

Tucked behind a discreet doorway in the
cocktail bar Dry Martini, it opens to reveal
one of Barcelona's best kept secrets: a
gourmet restaurant in a liquor warehouse.
The focus is on traditional seasonal food
done simply and well.
✉ Carrer d'Aribau 162 ☎ 93 217 5080
🕐 Mon–Fri 1–4:30, 8:30–midnight, Sat
8:30pm–midnight Ⓜ Hospital Clínic

Vino Tinto €€

This intimate Spanish steakhouse serves
"chuletons", thick, juicy charcoal-grilled
steak (similar to a T-bone) and succulent
morcilla and chorizo sausages, as well as a
dependable range of tapas and a selection
of wines.
✉ Carrer d'Aribau 27 ☎ 93 451 1027
🌐 www.vinotintoparrilla.com
🕐 Mon–Sat 1–4, 8:45–midnight
Ⓜ Universitat

Windsor €€€

This elegant dining room and pleasing
garden is aimed at discerning diners on big
budgets. Windsor offers over 400 wines
and dishes such as Catalan cannelloni with
wild mushrooms and truffles.
✉ Carrer de Còrsega 286 ☎ 93 415 8483
🌐 www.restaurantwindsor.com
🕐 Open Mon–Fri 1–4, 8:30–11,
Sat 8:30pm–11pm Ⓜ Diagonal

Shopping

Barcelona has witnessed a meteoric rise as a holiday destination and the world's commercial enterprises have started taking a renewed interest in the city's potential. Recent years have seen it become a popular Christmas shopping destination and the Tomb Bus – a blue bus that tours the flagship and designer stores of Passeig de Gràcia and Diagonal with convenient stops en route – ensures that the shops are easily accessible. But perhaps the most fun to be had is in exploring the small boutiques of fledgling designers and artists and making discoveries of your own. Whether your penchant is for food or fashion, art or antiques, interior design or crafts, Barcelona has it covered.

MONTJUÏC & RAVAL

Antidoto 28

A weird and wonderful world of light boxes, mounted collage, retro-punk clothes, quirky sculptures and all types of music – perfect for those who like to have an eclectic collection of things.

✉ Carrer de Ferlandia 28, El Raval
☎ 93 302 5271 ⓦⓦ www.vorticedesign.net
◉ Tue–Sat 11–2, 5–8:30 ⓠ Universitat, Sant Antoni

Barcelona Reykjavík

Pack your picnic hampers at this unlikely sounding bakery that offers hot-from-the-oven, 100 per cent organic bread and pastries daily.

✉ Carrer del Doctor Dou 12 ☎ 93 302 0921 ⓦⓦ www.barcelonareykjavik.com
◉ Mon–Fri 10–9, Sat 10–6 ⓠ Catalunya, Sant Antoni, Liceu

Camper

The Mallorcan shoemaker specialises in soft leather shoes and quirky designs ranging from sushi prints on sandals to psychedelic flower imprints on your soles.

✉ Plaça dels Àngels 6 ☎ 93 310 7222
ⓦⓦ www.camper.com ◉ Mon–Sat 10–10
ⓠ Universitat, Catalunya

Comité

This appealing store stocks new fashion by Europe's most promising upcoming designers. A great place to pick up shirts, skirts and gingham tops with ruche detailing. The designer labels here include Cecilia Sörensen and Martin Lamothe.

✉ Carrer del Notariat 8 ☎ 93 317 6883
ⓦⓦ www.comitebarcelona.com
◉ Mon–Sat noon–8:30 ⓠ Catalunya

Discos ó Castellò

A small but well-stocked music store covering every genre from rock and pop, to blues, jazz and classical. It's a good place to pick up good-quality Spanish records, and there are usually some interesting bargains on offer.

✉ Carrer dels Tallers 3 ☎ 93 302 5946
◉ Mon–Sat 10–1:30, 4:30–8
ⓠ Universitat

Giménez y Zuazo

This chic designer duo offers a wide range of clothes for the urban woman. Browse through sophisticated and colourful dresses, trendy shirts and trousers to find your style statement.

✉ Carrer d'Elisabets 20 ☎ 93 412 3381
ⓦⓦ www.gimenezzuazo.com
◉ Mon–Sat 10:30–3, 5–8:30
ⓠ Catalunya

Lailo

The classiest vintage shop on the famous "second-hand" street, Lailo is a treasure house of beautiful clothes spanning several decades and in some case centuries. It also stocks old costumes from the Liceu Opera House and the Palau de la Música for serious collectors. Velvet coats, elaborate dresses, leisure suits, antique riding coats, Chanel handbags – find some of the best vintage stuff here.

✉ Carrer de la Riera Baixa 20 ☎ 93 441 3749 ◉ Mon–Sat 11–2, 5–8:30 ⓠ Liceu

Siesta

This artistic wonderland stocks interesting ceramic sculptures, photographs of Barcelona and other exotic destinations, and high-quality paintings by artists from all over the world.

✉ Carrer de Ferlandia 18 El Raval
☎ 680 879157 ⓦⓦ www.siestaweb.com
◉ Tue–Sat 11–2, 5–8:30 ⓠ Universitat, Sant Antoni

Soul

A popular shop with an eclectic mix of funky French streetwear, collectqble vintage items and groovy accessories.

✉ Cqrrer dels Tallers 15 ☎ 93 481 3294
◉ Tue–Sat 10–2, 5–8:30 ⓠ Universitat

Vialis

One of Spain's best shoe shops with a fantastic range of supremely comfortable shoes such as long boots with clog-style soles, rubber stack heels and sandals. The styles are so ergonomic you'd think you were barefoot!

✉ Carrer d' Elisabets 20 ☎ 93 342 6071
🔳 www.vialis.es 🕐 Mon–Sat 10–1:30, 4:30–8 🚇 Catalunya

LAS RAMBLAS & BARRI GÒTIC

Adidas Originals

The sportswear giant's flagship store in the centre of the Barri Gòtic is a must for collectors of custom-made shell-toes, lollipop coloured "Candy" watches and seriously cool velour jumpsuits.

✉ Carrer d'Avinyó 6 ☎ 93 317 5579
🔳 www.adidas.es 🕐 Mon–Sat 10–9, Sun 10:30–9 🚇 Jaume I

Cacao Sampaka

This gourmet chocolate shop is the creation of Albert Adrià (pastry chef at El Bulli) who offers 100 per cent pure chocolate, as well as curiously flavoured bonbons such as anchovy and black olive.

✉ Carrer de Ferran 43–45 ☎ 93 304 1539
🔳 www.cacaosampaka.com 🕐 Mon–Sat 10–8:30 🚇 Liceu, Jaume I

Casa Gimeno

Barcelona's most famous cigar shop stocks everything a cigar aficionado could dream of, from zeppelin-shaped Cubanos to cellophane-wrapped Canary Island blunts.

✉ Las Ramblas 100 ☎ 93 318 4947
🔳 www.gimenocigars.com
🕐 Mon–Sat 10–1:30, 4:30–8:30
🚇 Catalunya

Formatgeria La Seu

Housed in Barcelona's first butter-making factory dating back to 1917. Scottish owner Katherine McLaughlin prides herself on

stocking only Spanish cheese. You can sample three with a glass of wine for under €3.

✉ Carrer de Dagueria 16 ☎ 93 412 6548
🔳 www.formatgerialaseu.com 🕐 Tue–Fri 10–2, 5–8 Sat 10–3, 5–8 🚇 Jaume I

L'Arca de l'Àvia

Besides stocking antique lace and linen, this iconic store houses exquisite vintage gowns and wedding dresses. The store has also supplied costumes for various films including the blockbuster *Titanic*.

✉ Carrer dels Banys Nous 20 ☎ 93 302 1598 🔳 www.larcadelavia.com
🕐 Mon–Fri 10–2, 5–8, Sat 11–2 🚇 Liceu

La Manual Alpargatera

The straw-soled shoes at La Manual Alpargatera mecca for espadrille lovers, are hand-made and custom-designed to suit individual tastes. Fans include Jack Nicholson and Michael Douglas.

✉ Carrer d'Avinyó 7 ☎ 93 301 0172
🔳 www.lamanualalpargatera.com
🕐 Tue–Sat 9:30–1:30, 4:30–8
🚇 Liceu

Mercat de la Boqueria

Arguably the most famous sight in Barcelona, the city's fresh produce market is a lively, colourful smorgasbord of fresh fish and seafood, garden-grown fruit, vegetables and delicious meat. Don't leave the city without sampling the wares at one of the markets bars.

✉ Las Ramblas 89 ☎ 93 318 2584
🔳 www.boqueria.info 🕐 Mon–Fri 8–830, Sat 8–8 🚇 Liceu

Mango

This global Spanish fashion chain offers a selection similar to that at Zara. It's worth checking out both stores while on a shopping spree. On offer are basic T-shirts, cotton trousers, fashionable skirts and dresses, a great selection of chic accessories, bags and shoes.

⊠ Avinguda Portal de l'Angel
☎ 93 317 6985 ⓦ www.mango.es
🕙 Mon–Sat 10–9 🚇 Catalunya

Papabubble

A retro sweet shop, Papabubble specialises in home-made boiled candy in all colours (and flavours) of the rainbow. This Ozzie-run outlet has some unique offerings, from traditional mint humbugs and sticks of rock with your name to cheeky body part sculptures.

⊠ **Carrer de la Dagueria 16** ☎ 93 268 8625
ⓦ www.papabubble.com
🕙 Tue–Fri 10–2, 4–8:30, Sat 10–8:30, Sun 11–7:30 🚇 Barceloneta, Drassanes

Zara

With branches scattered all over the city, this famous European store is a staple for fashion-conscious Catalans who come here for day-to-day basics as well as more glamorous evening garb. It has trendy clothes for men, women and children, and a street fashion department. There is also a good home department – Zara Home.

⊠ Avinguda del Portal de l'Àngel 24 and 34
☎ 93 317 4452 ⓦ www.zara.com
🕙 Mon–Sat 10–7 🚇 Catalunya

PORT VELL & LA RIBERA

Arlequí Mascares

The walls of this store are lined with interesting masks crafted from papier mâché and leather. Whether you have a penchant for sequined masks, traditional Japanese or Catalan one, gorgeous or grotesque masks, chances are you'll find it here.

⊠ **Carrer de la Princesa 7** ☎ 93 268 2752
ⓦ www.arlequimask.com 🕙 Mon–Sat 10:30–8:30, Sun 10:30–4:30 🚇 Jaume I

Casa Gisbert

Come to this aromatic dried goods store to stock up on freshly roasted coffee, top-grade Spanish almonds, hazelnuts, artisan jams and candied fruit.

⊠ **Carrer dels Sombrerers 23** ☎ 93 319 7535 ⓦ www.casagispert.com 🕙 Tue–Fri 9:30–2, 4–7:30, Sat 10–2, 5–8 🚇 Jaume I

Custo Barcelona

The Custo Brothers' distinctive and flamboyant T-shirt designs, ranging from psychedelic flowers to people, are among the most recognised brands from Barcelona. The range now spans coats, trousers and skirts.

⊠ **Plaça de les Olles 7** ☎ 93 268 7893
ⓦ www.custo-barcelona.com
🕙 Mon–Sat 10–10 🚇 Jaume I

Declivelan

Declivelan houses an intriguing and eclectic range of jewellery by Alberto Gomez called "Nicotine", and the shop also stocks a complimentary clothing by Pablo Martinez, a young Basque designer.

⊠ **Carrer de Grunyí 6** ☎ 93 310 2484
ⓦ www.nicotineordie.com 🕙 Mon–Sat 10–2, 5–8 🚇 Jaume I

Ici et Là

A quirky interiors store stocking a delightful collection of home wares including chandeliers fashioned from semi-precious stones, floor cushions in a variety of colours and funky chairs.

⊠ **Plaça Santa María del Mar 2**
☎ 93 268 1167 🕙 Mon 4:30–8:30, Tue–Sat 10:30–8:30 🚇 Jaume I

Maremagnum

This rather striking shopping mall, situated in the middle of Port Vell, has undergone a dramatic transformation in the last couple of years. Today it's a trendy hot spot housing high-street chains, swanky new bars, restaurants and even the Barcelona Football Team shop.

⊠ **Moll d'Espanya s/n** ☎ 93 225 8100
ⓦ www.maremagnum.es
🕙 Daily 10–10 🚇 Drassanes

Origen 99.9%

For anyone in doubt about what authentic gourmet products to take home, this place provides an easy one-stop shop specialising in all things Catalan. For some tasty cultural education try the meaty, pea-sized *arbequina* olives, artisan *cava* (Catalan champagne) and mountain goat cheese. All outlets have restaurants attached.

✉ Passeig del Born 4 ☎ 93 295 6690
🖥 www.origen99.com ⏰ Mon–Thu 8:30–7, Fri 8–2 Ⓜ Jaume I

Rafa Teja Atelier

For exclusive silk and pashmina scarves as well as the more traditional Spanish lace shawls, look no further than this specialist boutique.

✉ Carrer de Santa Maria 18 ☎ 93 310 2785 ⏰ Mon–Sat 11–9 Ⓜ Jaume I

Urban Eccentric

A small store, specialising in smart leather Lupo handbags made in Barcelona. True craftsmen use the highest quality materials to fashion these beautiful pieces.

✉ Carrer de Esquirol 4 ☎ 93 268 7221
🖥 www.urbaneccentric.tv ⏰ Tue–Sat 10–1:30, 4:30–8:30 Ⓜ Jaume I

Vila Viniteca

The old city's premier wine shop sells top-class wines from all over Spain, as well as liqueurs and traditional fire waters. Across the road, the company has recently opened a small, upmarket tasting room and delicatessen.

✉ Carrer dels Agullers 7 ☎ 93 268 3227
🖥 www.vilaviniteca.es ⏰ Mon–Sat 8:30–2:30, 4:30–8:30, closed Sat evenings in winter Ⓜ Jaume I

L'EIXAMPLE

Antonio Pernas

The Spanish designer from A Coruña makes beautiful clothes for dressy occasions. The 2007–2008 season collection is a riot of statement-making gold frocks and smocks, silk evening suits and pretty summer dresses. The more young and colourful Agatha Ruiz de la Prada is situated in the same building.

✉ Carrer del Consell de Cent 314–316
☎ 93 487 1667 🖥 www.antonio-permas.es
⏰ Mon–Sat 10–8 Ⓜ Passeig de Gràcia

Cache–Cache

Bright, fun clothes for toddlers as well as for older children. It also has a great range of maternity wear.

✉ Carrer de Valencia 282 ☎ 93 215 4007
⏰ Mon–Sat 10–8:30 Ⓜ Passeig de Gràcia

Colmado Quílez

Take home sumptuous conserved vegetables such as own-brand *piquillo* peppers and silky white asparagus, luxury cheeses and charcuterie, preserves and sweetmeats, smoked salmon and caviar from this gourmet paradise located in Eixample's most stunning turn-of-the-20th-century store.

✉ Rambla de Catalunya 63
☎ 93 215 2356 ⏰ Mon–Sat 10–2, 5–8
Ⓜ Passeig de Gràcia

Comptoir des Cotonniers

This French chain makes sophisticated, baby-soft cotton clothing for mothers and daughters. Cute gingham smocks, feather light T-shirts and cute yet daring printed baby-grows are worth picking up.

✉ Carrer de Consell de Cent 302 ☎ 93 467 2874 🖥 www.comptoirdescotonniers. com ⏰ Mon–Sat 10–8:30 Ⓜ Passeig de Gràcia

El Corte Inglés

Spain's premier department store stocking everything from gourmet foods to fashion brands and exquisite china. There's also a restaurant on the top floor with great views. Another large El Corte Inglés can be found only a few minutes' walk from this store on Avinguda del Portal De l'Angel, about halfway down the street.

✉ Plaça de Catalunya 14 ☎ 93 306 3800 🖥 www.elcorteingles.es 🕐 Mon–Sat 10–10 🚇 Catalunya

Els Encants Flea Market

On the whole, Barcelona is not one for quality second-hand goods or antiques, with the notable exception of Els Encants. Its official name is La Feria de Bellcaire – a Parisian-style flea market that dates back to the 14th century. Today it has more than 1,000 stalls, much of it junk, but there are still some treasures if you dig deep enough. The best bargains surface early in the morning.

✉ Carrer del Dos de Maig 186, Plaça Glòries Catalanes 1 ☎ 93 246 3030 🕐 Mon, Wed, Fri and Sat 9–8 🚇 Glòries

Groc

Great designer creations for both men and women from popular Catalonian designer Toni Mirò.

✉ Rambla de Catalunya 100bis ☎ 93 215 0180 🕐 Mon–Sat 10:30–8:30, 4:30–8:30 🚇 Diagonal

Hibernian Books

A real treat for literary lovers, Hibernian has a vast collection of English-language books in every genre. It also has a kids's section and some second-hand tomes.

✉ Carrer de Pere Serafí 33–35 ☎ 93 217 4796 🖥 www.hibernian-books.com 🚇 Fontana

Janina

A great place to shop for ultra-feminine lingerie and enticing nightwear. Some of the well-known brands include Christian Dior, La Perla and Lacroix. It also offers large-size options and a very useful next-day alteration service.

✉ Rambla de Catalunya 94 ☎ 93 215 0484 🕐 Mon–Sat 🚇 Provenca

L'Appartement

This store is the last word in interior design with bold art, trendy table lamps and distinctive candles. The aim is to promote the work of young designers and to ensure that shoppers walk away with something unique. Each month a new talent is promoted, such as Japanese designer Hiroshi Tsunoda.

✉ Carrer de'Enric Granados 44 ☎ 93 452 2904 🖥 www.lappartement.es 🕐 Mon–Sat 10:30–3, 4:30–9, Sat 10:30–2, 5–9 🚇 Fontana

L'Illa Diagonal

Designed by architects Rafael Moneo and Manuel de Solà-Morales to resemble New York's Rockerfeller Center lying down, this shopping mall is home to the city's top brands and has a world-class food court.

✉ Avinguda Diagonal 545–557 ☎ 93 306 3800 🖥 www.lilla.com 🕐 Mon–Sat 10–9:30 🚇 Maria Cristina

Purificación García

This designer store offers Purificación's sleek, sophisticated creations. The understated designs for men are jazzed up with a wide palette of colours and inventive use of fabrics; the slightly more whimsical women's styles effortlessly flirt with bohemian chic. This is a good place to shop for cotton shirts in a range of colours, well-tailored suits and stylish ties.

✉ Passeig de Gràcia 21 ☎ 93 487 7292 🖥 www.purificaciongarcia.es 🕐 Mon–Sat 10–8:30 🚇 Passeig de Gràcia

TDM (Tienda de Moda)

Drop in here for a great selection of Spanish as well as international designer wear, including all the top names such as Armani, Armand Basi and Gucci, among many others. This is the flagship store, but there are several other outlets in the city.

✉ Carrer Gran de Gràcia 106 ☎ 93 217 4971 🕐 Mon–Sat 10–8:30 🚇 Passeig de Gràcia

Entertainment

Barcelona is a city that likes to party. People go out late, often meeting for drinks around 10 or later, and stay out till the early hours. Generally bars stay open until about 3am, which is when many of the top nightclubs open and keep going until dawn. The scene is fun, friendly and varied, offering a mix of laid-back lounge bars, New York-style cocktail bars, sultry ballrooms and mega dance clubs. For those who prefer to get their kicks while the sun is still up, there are plenty of daytime diversions too, ranging from bicycle tours to relaxation in a spa.

MONTJUÏC & RAVAL

Artists Love Barcelona

This smart art studio is located near the MACBA in El Raval and offers daily, weekend and weeklong courses in English and Spanish. Most courses are in Barcelona and cover painting, photography, life drawing and languages, striking the perfect balance between entertainment and education.

✉ Carrer de Ferlandia 26 ☎ 93 302 2779
ⓦ www.artistslovebarcelona.com
Ⓜ Sant Antoni, Universitat

Bar Xix

A former dairy, Bar Xix still boasts its original fixtures and fittings, including a carved bar and marble table tops. Today visitors willingly cross town for the city's best gin and tonics and a wide range of other cocktails.

✉ Carrer de Rocafort 19 ☎ 93 423 4314
ⓦ www.xixbar.com ⏰ Mon–Sat 6:30pm–1:30am (also 9am–4:30pm) Ⓜ Poble Sec

Caribbean Club

This clandestine cocktail bar usually looks closed but rarely is. Secreted behind hobbit-sized wooden doors the bar offers drinks that are generally bigger and better than those at the more famous Boadas around the corner.

✉ Carrer de les Sitges 5 ☎ 93 302 2182
⏰ Tue–Sat 7pm–2am Ⓜ Catalunya

Giggling Guiri

Dark, intimate and always game for a laugh, this cabaret-style club is the city's only stand-up comedy venue. Attracting a stellar line-up of British comedians, this is a great place to have an evening of fun and laughter. Tickets cost €15 in advance, €17 on the door.

✉ Teatro Llantiol, Carrer de la Riereta 7
☎ 93 329 9009 ⓦ www.gigglingguiri.com
Ⓜ Sant Antoni, Paral.lel

Marsella

Barcelona's legendary absinthe bar dates back to 1865 and evidently hasn't changed much since. Frequented by legends like Picasso and Miró in the past it still retains its charming atmosphere. Murky booze bottles and dusty chandeliers merely serve to add to the ambience when you dance with the little green fairy.

✉ Carrer de Sant Pau 65 ☎ 93 442 7263
⏰ Mon–Thu 10pm–2am, Fri–Sat 10pm–3am
Ⓜ Paral.lel, Liceu

Resolis

The only bar on the "vintage/second hand" street, Resolis recently got a make-over, keeping its century old heritage intact. It

offers good tapas and a full range of wines by the glass. The terrace has some great views in mid-summer.

✉ Carrer de la Riera Baixa 22 ☎ 93 441 2948 ⏰ Mon–Thu 11am–midnight, Fri–Sat 11am–2am

Sala Apolo

The faded grandeur of this former ball-room makes a great nightclub, with clubbers grooving to different genres of music. Whether your preference is funk, soul or reggae, Apolo generally has something for every mood.

✉ Nou de la Rambla 113 ☎ 93 301 0090
ⓦ www.sala-apolo.com ⏰ Wed–Sat 12:30am–5am, Sun 10:30pm–3am
Ⓜ Paral.lel

LAS RAMBLAS & BARRI GÒTIC

Club 13

This upmarket nightspot is the full package, offering night owls a mezzanine restaurant with traditional tapas on the extensive menu, a terrace on the plaza, and a trendy basement disco complete with mirrored walls and black leather sofas.

✉ Plaça Reial 13 ☎ 93 412 4327
⏰ Mon–Thu, Sun 2pm–2:30am, Fri–Sat 6pm–3am
Ⓜ Liceu

Fat Tire Bike Tours

With branches in Paris and Berlin, Fat Tire Bike Tours are veterans in offering tours of the city by bike. They pride themselves on details such as comfortably cushioned seats and chunky tyres. The pace is relaxed, there are no hills to climb and there is even a break on the beach. Guided tours last four hours and give a good all-round perspective of the city.

✉ C/Escudellers 48 ☎ 93 301 3612
ⓦ www.fattirebiketoursbarcelona.com
⏰ Mar to Dec, daily 11am; enquire for additional tours in high season
Ⓜ Liceu, Drassanes, Jaume I

Ginger

Smart and sexy with a cocktail bar at one end, a wine bar at the other and white armchairs in the middle, Ginger draws a diverse crowd of people.

✉ Carrer de la Palma de Sant Just 1
☎ 93 310 5309 🕐 Tue–Thu 7pm–2.30am, Fri–Sat 7pm–3am 🚇 Jaume I

Jamboree

A popular live music venue that gets fairly outrageous on its club nights. The music can be wonderful, ranging from world-class jazz sessions to more contemporary rhythm 'n' blues.

✉ Plaça Reial 17 ☎ 93 319 1789
🆆 www.masimas.com/jamboree
🕐 Call for times 🚇 Liceu

Gran Teatre del Liceu

Barcelona's spectacular gilded opera house was destroyed by a fire in 1861, had two bombs thrown into the stalls in 1893 that killed 20 people, and was destroyed by fire again in 1994. However, it continues to stand strong, as does the people's passion for their opera house. Extensive refurbishments following this most recent disaster have upgraded it to a world-class venue in terms of audio visual technology, while maintaining the breathtaking interior. The Petit Liceu is specifically a children's opera.

✉ Las Ramblas 51–59 ☎ 93 485 9913
🆆 www.liceubarcelona.com
🕐 Mon–Fri 11–2, 3–8; box office Mon–Fri 2–8:30
🚇 Liceu

PORT VELL & LA RIBERA

CDLC

Based on the Supper Club in Amsterdam, day beds in the dining room may be nothing new but they still draw a crowd who like to see and be seen, including members of Barcelona's football team. The seafront chill-out area is another major

bonus. Book your bed in advance.

✉ Passeig Marítim 32 ☎ 93 224 0470
🆆 www.cdlcbarcelona.com
🕐 Mon–Wed noon–2:30am, Thu–Sun noon–3am 🚇 Ciutadella-Vila Olímpica, Barceloneta

Club Mix

A heady cocktail of acid jazz, neo soul, rare grove and electric boogaloo, Club Mix is where people go to party mid-week to the anthems of the city's finest DJs. The 1970s style, cushioned banquettes and disco balls give it a retro sparkle.

✉ Carrer del Comerç 21 ☎ 93 319 4696
🆆 www.clubmixbcn.com 🕐 Wed–Sat from 11pm 🚇 Barceloneta, Jaume I

Diobar

The colourful decor and upbeat atmosphere of this basement club, the new home of Café Royale, attracts a grown-up crowd of disco divas who favour funk and Motown, lounge and deep house over hip-hop and techno.

✉ Underneath Dionisos restaurant, Avinguda Marquès d'Argentera 27 baixos (in front of the Estació Francia) ☎ 93 319 5619
🆆 www.diobar.net 🕐 Thu–Sat 10pm–3am
🚇 Barceloneta, Jaume I

Gimlet

Small and narrow, there's not much breathing space in Gimlet (named for the potent gin-based cocktail that's its speciality), but it's fabulous enough that nobody cares. Arrive early to ensure you have a seat at the polished wood bar.

✉ Carrer del Rec 24 ☎ 93 310 1027
🕐 Daily 7pm–3am 🚇 Jaume I

Luz de Gas

Join the glitterati on this permanently moored party boat at the top of Port Vell. Spilling over onto an exclusive terrace, the champagne starts flowing mid-afternoon and doesn't stop until the small hours.

✉ Moll del Diposit s/n ☎ 93 484 2326

📧 www.luzdegas.com 🕐 Daily noon–3am; closed Nov–Mar 🚇 Barceloneta

Mondo Club

A newcomer to the Maremagnum end of the port where traditionally nothing much happens, Mondo oozes glamour. The city's trendy crowd can be seen lounging around on lipstick-red sofas at this part-restaurant, part-club before hitting party sessions by Hotel Costes and Hed Kandi.

📧 Maremagnum, Moll d'Espanya s/n
📞 93 221 3911 📧 www.mondobcn.com
🕐 Wed–Sun 1pm–3am 🚇 Drassanes

Yelmo Icària Cineplex

This is the biggest original version cinema complex in Barcelona with several screens and state-of-the-art technology. While the area itself lacks character, it is a safe bet for catching the latest blockbuster.

📧 Carrer de Salvador Espriú 61, Vila Olímpica 📞 93 221 7585
📧 www.yelmocineplex.es
🚇 Ciutadella-Vila Olímpica

L'EIXAMPLE

A mà Teràpies

Chilled out and cheerful, A mà Teràpies is run by Irish native Pamela Thompson who has more than 20 years experience in the well-being industry and counts Joan Collins among past clients. The treatments include Thai massage, deluxe facials and pedicures.

📧 Carrer d'Enric Granados 23, 2º-2ª
📞 93 451 6572 📧 www.amaterapies.org 🕐 Mon–Sat 10–10, Sun noon–6
🚇 Universitat

Buda Restaurante

The downtown lair of models and minor celebrities, Buda is all about putting on the ritz. With its retro wallpaper, sparkling chandeliers and upbeat mood, it attracts a charismatic crowd of Barcelona's bright young things. If you want to make a night

of it, the restaurant serves decent, modern Mediterranean fare.

📧 Carrer de Pau Claris 92 📞 93 318 4252
📧 www.budabarcelona.com
🕐 Daily 9pm–3am 🚇 Catalunya

Chaise Lounge

A groovy little place that has live music most nights. Break out the guitar on Tuesdays to join the jam sessions, chill to Brazilian bossa nova on Thursdays and groove to pop tunes of the 1980s and 1990s on Saturday.

📧 Carrer de la Diputació 2006 📞 93 323 2235 🕐 Mon 8am–10pm, Tue–Fri 8am–3am, Sat 10pm–3am 🚇 Universitat

Danzatoria

This glamorous mansion house lounge-club in the upper reaches of Barcelona, is spread over several levels and encompasses dance floors, chill-out lounges and sleek, palm-filled terraces.

📧 Avinguda del Tibidabo 61 Barcelona
📞 93 211 6261 📧 www.danzatoria-barcelona.com 🕐 Tue–Sat 9pm–2:30am, Sun 8pm–2:30am 🚇 Avenida Tibidabo

Sala Razzmatazz

Razz invites established British Indie bands, as well as newcomers to play in this state-of-the-art warehouse. Once the music is done, five night clubs and six bars ensure the party doesn't stop there.

📧 Carrer dels Almogàvers 122 📞 93 320 8200 📧 www.salarazzmatazz.com 🕐 Fri–Sat 1am–5am (club nights); check website for live music schedule 🚇 Bogatell, Marina

Shadow Lounge Bar

It was only a matter of time before Tokyo's lauded "Oxygen" bars made their debut here. This one offers 15-minute flavoured oxygen blasts to keep you going through Barcelona's infamously late nights.

📧 Carrer del Consell de Cent 223 📞 93 452 4712 📧 www.shadowloungebar.com
🕐 Wed–Thu and Sun 8pm–2:30am, Fri–Sat 10pm–3am 🚇 Urgell

Travel Facts

Barcelona is a thrilling holiday destination. The city is crammed with historic sights, architectural marvels, museums and lively bars and cafés. To make your way around the city more easily there are certain practical details that you will need to know. This section will give you all the information to make your holiday a success – from getting around in the city to advice on currency, climate, discounts, health services and much more.

ARRIVING

Barcelona's airport is El Prat (tel: 902 40 4 704; www.aena.es) located 11km (7 miles) southwest of Barcelona. To get to the centre, a taxi costs around €25. The blue Aerobús (tel: 93 415 6020) runs from each terminal to Plaça de Cataluyna passing Plaça de'Espanya, Carrer Urgell and Plaça de la Universitat on the way. A single ticket is €3.75 and a return (valid for one week) is €6.45. The journey takes around 30 minutes and buses leave the airport around every 10 minutes 6am–1am on weekdays and 6:30am–1am on weekends.

To travel by train take the overhead walkway between terminals A and B to the train station. The C10 leaves the airport every 30 minutes 6am–11:44pm and the journey takes 20–30 minutes. A single ticket costs €2.50 or you can use the T-10 card if you already have one (see Getting Around opposite).

CALENDAR OF EVENTS

The main public holiday in Barcelona is the feast day of the city's patron saint, La Mercè, on 24 September, which involves a week-long party with *gegants* (giant costumed processional figures), free music concerts, human castles, fireworks, parades and the riotous *correfoc* – a "fire run" with fire-breathing dragons and impish devils. Other big events are Sónar in June, a three-day festival of electronic music (www.sonar. es); the summer Grec theatre festival, and the summer solstice celebrations for Sant Joan on the night of 23 June. For children, the main events are Santa Eulàlia on 12 February and, of course, the frenzy of gift buying that accompanies Nadal (Christmas) and the arrival of the Reis (Three Kings) on 6 January. For a comprehensive calendar of events see the city council's website www.bcn.es.

CLIMATE

Barcelona has an enviable climate, with long, hot summers and cool winters. The ideal months to visit are May and June or September and October, when the weather is sunny and dry but not overpoweringly hot. In August, locals desert Barcelona for the coastal resorts to escape the heat and humidity. April and November are often very wet, although still quite warm and mild. January is the coldest month, with top temperatures averaging 13°C (55°F), while August is the hottest, with an average high of 29°C (84°F).

CLOTHING

Barcelona is a very fashionable, stylish city and visitors will feel more comfortable if they make a bit of an effort. If you want to blend in, note that local men over the age of 40 or so do not generally wear shorts, and even in the Barceloneta area, once off the sandy beaches it is not really acceptable to wander around in swimming trunks or bikinis; you will certainly not be allowed into any bars or restaurants dressed like this.

When visiting churches or the cathedral, women must cover their shoulders and knees and men must remove their hats.

In restaurants, dress is usually informal and even in top-notch establishments, a jacket and tie is not obligatory. Nightclubs are ferociously trendy, but also pretty informal and many clubbers party the night away in jeans and trainers; however, if you want to muscle your way past the bouncers on a busy night it is wise to make an effort.

CUSTOMS

The limits for non-EU visitors are 200 cigarettes, or 50 cigars, or 250g (9 ounces) of tobacco; 1 litre (0.02 gallons) of spirits (over 22 per cent), or 2 litres (0.04 gallons) of fortified wine, 2 litres (0.04 gallons) of still wine; 50g (2 ounces) of perfume. The guidelines for EU residents (for personal use) are 3,200 cigarettes, 200 cigars, 1kg (35 ounces) tobacco; 10 litres (2.6 gallons) of spirits (over 22 per cent), 20 litres (5.2 gallons) of aperitifs, 90 litres (23 gallons) of wine, of which 60 can be sparkling, 110 litres (29 gallons) of beer; 50g (2 ounces) of perfume.

Visitors under 17 are not entitled to the tobacco and alcohol allowances.

DRIVING

Driving in Barcelona is frustrating and expensive. Parking is even more so. If you must drive, remember that it is obligatory to carry your driving licence, vehicle registration and insurance documents with you at all times. EU visitors can generally drive with a valid driving licence from their country (the older green paper UK licence is officially accepted, but may not be familiar to all traffic officers). For more detailed information check the Ministry of the Interior's website www.dgt.es.

Parking in the city is nightmarishly complicated, so try to use official underground car parks (parking is marked by a large white P on a square blue sign) wherever possible; the cost is around €2.35 an hour.

If the police tow your car away, they leave a triangular sticker on the kerb, which should let you know where to pick it up, or tel: 090

236 4116. Most petrol stations have regular (*super*), unleaded (*sense plom/sin plomo*) and diesel (*gas-oil*).

ELECTRICITY

The standard electrical current in Spain is 220V. Plug sockets take two-round-pin plugs, so an adaptor is necessary for British three-pin electrical items. US (110V) equipment will require a current transformer in addition to an adaptor.

EMBASSIES AND CONSULATES

The British and United States embassies are in Madrid.

British Consulate

Avinguda Diagonal 477 13th floor, Eixample
Tel: 93 366 6200; www.ukinspain.com
Open mid-September to mid-June, Mon–Fri 9:30am–2pm; mid-June to mid-September 8:30am–1:30pm.

US Consulate

Passeig de la Reina Elisenda 23, Zona Alta
Tel: 93 280 2227; www.embusa.es
Open Mon–Fri 9am–1pm.

GETTING AROUND

Barcelona's public transport (www.tmb.net) is efficient and more integrated than ever, with the same tickets for bus, tram, local train and metro. There is a flat fare of €1.30 per journey, but a T-10 card (T deu/T diez) offers better value at €6.90 for 10 rides in Zone 1. The T-10 card can be shared and also allows up to four free transfers between transport systems within 75 minutes of the start of the journey; simply pass your card through the machine and no more units will be deducted. T-10s are sold in newsagents and Servi-Caixa cashpoints as well as the metro and train stations, but not on the buses. Also useful for visitors is the Barcelona Card, which allows unlimited use of public transport for up to five days; it is sold at tourist offices, the airport and through www.barcelonaturisme.com.

Barcelona's black and yellow taxis can be hailed on the street or from taxi ranks when the taxi has a green light on the roof and a sign on the windscreen saying *lliure/libre* (free). The tariffs are posted on the rear passenger window in Catalan, Spanish and English, with information on surcharges for luggage, airport and port transfers and Saturday nights and holidays. Note that taxi drivers are not required to change any note larger than €20 and do not usually take credit cards.

HEALTH FACILITIES

For anything that is not urgent it is usually quicker to rely on private travel insurance than the state healthcare system. For emergency attention call 061 for an ambulance or head to the casualty department (*Urgències/Urgencias*) of any of the main public hospitals. All are open 24 hours daily. Some of the most central are Hospital del Mar (Passeig Marítim 25–29, Barceloneta, tel: 93 248 3000; Metro Ciutadella-Vila Olímpica), Hospital Clínic (Carrer de Villaroel 170, Eixample tel: 93 227 5400; Metro Hospital Clínic). For details about entitlement to free emergency healthcare check the website www.gencat. net/temes/eng/salut.htm or call the 24-hour health information line on tel: 090 211 1444. EU Nationals are entitled to free medical care if they have the European Health Insurance Card (EHIC) which is valid for one year.

LANGUAGE

Barcelona is a completely bilingual city and although many locals prefer to speak Catalan (*català*) they can all speak and understand Spanish, which is generally referred to as *castellà/castellano* rather than *espanyol/español*. Catalan is the dominant everyday language of over a third of Barcelona residents and nearly 90 per cent understand it. A few phrases of Catalan go a long way with locals who are accustomed to switching to English or at least Spanish when dealing with visitors. Most road signs and all street names are in Catalan, and in

most written documents, from restaurant menus to museum labels you will find Catalan first, then Spanish.

MONEY MATTERS

The currency in Spain is the euro (€); each euro is divided into 100 cents (*céntims/céntimos*) while notes come in denominations of €500, €200, €100, €50, €20, €10 and €5. All but the biggest establishments are reluctant to take notes larger than €50; good places to break large notes are metro stations and hotels.

Major credit cards are accepted in most establishments, including public transport ticket machines, and many European debit cards can also be used.

Note that photo ID is necessary when using a credit card in a shop (but not restaurants) and that more and more places are introducing chip and pin machines at the counter or check out.

Banks and savings banks are generally open from 8:30am to 2pm Monday to Friday, and in the winter some also open on Saturday mornings and Thursday afternoons. They usually accept euro travellers' cheques for a commission and tend to offer better rates than the exchange offices. The easiest option is to use one of the thousands of ATMs with a debit or credit card.

OPENING HOURS

Most museums close on Sunday afternoons and Mondays.

All-day opening (10am to 8pm) is becoming the norm for larger shops and chains, particularly those in central Barcelona. Smaller shops generally open from around 10am to 2pm and then 5pm to 8pm Monday to Saturday. Sunday opening is limited to some public holidays, mostly in the run up to Christmas, and to shops in tourist zones such as the Ramblas and the Maremagnum commercial centre. The 40 or so municipal markets open at 7am or 8am and close at 2pm; most also open on Friday afternoons from 5pm to 8pm.

Many shops, restaurants and businesses close down completely for at least two weeks in July or August.

POSTAL SERVICES

There are post offices (*correus/correos*) all over town: look for a yellow sign with a curling blue or white horn insignia. The central office is at Plaça d'Antoni López, Barri Gòtic (tel: 93 486 8050; open Mon–Fri 8:30am–9:30pm, Sat 8:30am–2pm). Take a numbered ticket from the machines by the entrance and wait for your turn. Additional services include money transfer, fax sending and receiving and Burofax courier delivery. Queues can be long and it can be very slow.

Post boxes in the street are yellow with two slots, one for the city (marked *ciutat*) and one for outside Barcelona. Stamps (*sellos*) are sold in government-run tobacco shops (*estanc/estanco*); letters and postcards weighing up to 20g (0.7 ounces) cost 30 cents within Spain; 58 cents to the rest of Europe; 78 cents to the rest of the world; for further information check the post office website www.correos.es. Post generally takes around five working days to the rest of Europe and eight to ten days to the US.

SECURITY

Barcelona is not a violent or dangerous city but it does have a terrible reputation for pickpocketing and bag-snatching. Tourists are the main targets, and areas such as the Ramblas, central Metro stations, the beach, the park and the airport are real hot spots.

To avoid making yourself a target, observe the following tips: leave extra money, expensive equipment, important documents and other valuables in your hotel safe; keep your money in a zipped inside pocket; when you stop for lunch or coffee keep your bags on your lap, not on the floor or the back of your chair; avoid unlit streets at night; move away immediately if someone gets too close or acts suspiciously when, say, asking for directions or selling "lucky" herbs.

TELEPHONE NUMBERS AND CODES

Landlines and mobile numbers have nine digits. Mobile numbers begin with a 6 and landline numbers in Barcelona province always begin with the area code 93. Local and national calls to standard landlines are free, although numbers starting 90 are special-rate services and can be expensive.

To make an international call dial 00, then the country code, followed by the area code (omitting the first 0 in UK numbers) and then the number. To phone Spain from abroad, dial 00, followed by 34 followed by the number.

Public payphones are notoriously vandalised or simply malfunctioning, but if you want to try your luck, you can pay with coins, credit cards and special phone cards which you can buy at the tobacco stores or newsagents. For the first minute of a local call you'll pay around 8 cents; around 14 cents to a mobile.

To use your mobile (*móvil*) in Spain, check rates with your service provider before you leave: some packages charge to receive calls abroad or charge international roaming rates even for local calls. If using a US phone, check for GSM compatibility. Long-term visitors might find it cheaper to buy a pay-as-you-go package from local phone stores which can be

topped up at cash machines, newsagents and tobacco stores (*estancs/estancos*). The three major firms are Movistar (www. movistar.es), Vodafone (www.vodafone.es) and Orange (www.orange.es).

Another option is to use the phone centres (*locutorios*) full of small phone booths offering cheap international calls. There are many of these centres in the Raval, particularly along Carrer de Sant Pau, and Carrer de l'Hospital and also along Carrer dels Carders in the Born. General information in Barcelona: 010 (8am–10pm Mon–Sat; English-speaking operators are available although you may have to wait).

National directory enquiries: 11818
International directory enquiries: 11825
Telefónica: 1004

TIPPING

Tipping is generally left to personal discretion and there is certainly no pressure to leave huge tips in any situation. It is customary to tip hotel porters, and in taxis most passengers just round up the fare to the nearest euro, especially if the driver has been helpful with luggage. If you have a drink while seated at the bar it is acceptable to just leave a few coins. For a sit-down meal in a restaurant it is fair to leave around 5–10 per cent for the staff, although many Catalans (who have a reputation for being a little careful with their money) will quite

unashamedly leave a few small coins or even nothing at all. If the service is very poor, you should not feel pressured to leave a tip – waiters earn a fixed wage and do not rely on tips as they do in the United States.

TOURIST OFFICES

The main office is located underground at Plaça de Catalunya (tel: 93 285 3834; www. bcn.es/www.barcelonaturisme.com; open daily 9am–9pm) just across from El Corte Inglés department store, and has information desks, ticket sales for museums, shows and transport, a hotel booking service, a book and souvenir shop and currency exchange. Other offices are located in the airport; La Rambla 115; Carrer de la Ciutat 2 on the ground floor of the Ajuntament building in Plaça de Sant Jaume; Plaça del Portal de la Pau in front of the Columbus monument; and Sants train station.

The information centre of the city's culture department, the Centre d'Informació de la Virreina (Palau de la Virreina, Las Ramblas 99, tel: 93 316 1000; www.bcn.es/cultura; open Mon–Sat 10–8, Sun 11–3) has details of shows, exhibitions and other cultural events along with a good bookstore. The Generalitat's information centre, the Centre d'Informació de Catalunya (Palau Robert, Passeig de Gràcia 107, tel: 93 238 8091; www.gencat.net/probert; open Mon–Sat 10–7, Sun 10–2:30) has a host of brochures, books and maps for all of Catalonia.

Index

A

accommodation 162-165
airport 184
Ajuntament 72, 73
amusement park 154-155
Antoni Tàpies Foundation 118
Aquarium 103
Arc de Triompf 97
Archaeological Museum 29
Las Arenas 37, 42
art courses 178-179
ATMs 186

B

Baja Beach Club 100-101
banks 186
Barcelona chair 41
Barcelona Contemporary Art
   Museum 16, 30-31
Barceloneta 80, 82-85, 101
Barri Gòtic 48-51
bars 179, 180, 181
beaches 84, 101, 159
bike tours 179
Black Virgin 144
Block of Discord see Manzana de
   la Discordia
Boqueria 75-76, 174
El Bosc de les Fades 57
Botanical Garden 26-27
buses and trams 185

C

cable car 19, 104
Café Zurich 63, 112
Caixaforum 16, 18
Capella de Sant Jordi 73
Capella de Santa Agatha 68
Capilla de Sant Cristóbal 51
Carrer Bisbe 72
Carrer Ciutat 72, 73
Carrer Ferran 72
Carrer Jaume I 72
Carrer Merce 49
Casa Amattler 125-126
Casa Battló 114, 125, 126
Casa Lleó-Morera 125
Casa Milà 112, 114-117
Casa Padellas 68
Casa dels Paraigües 77
Castel dels Tres Dragons 97
Castell de Montjuïc 18, 19
Catedral, Barcelona 46, 52-55
Catedral, Tarragona 159
Cau Ferrat 156

Centre d'Art Santa Mònica 77
Ceramics Museum 153
Chocolate Museum 80, 89
churches
Capella de Sant Jordi 73
Capella de Santa Agatha 68
Capilla de Sant Cristóbal 51
Catedral, Barcelona 46, 52-55
Catedral, Tarragona 159
Església de la Mercè 49, 64
Sagrada Familia 136-141
Sagrat Cor 155
Sant Paul del Camp 43
Santa Maria del Mar 106-109
Santa Maria del Pi 49, 65
cinemas 103, 121, 181
City History Museum 68
climate and seasons 184
Cloud and Chair (Tàpies) 118
clubs 178, 179, 180, 181
Collegi d'Arquitectes 51
comedy venue 179
concerts 55, 94-95, 109
Consell de Cent 73
El Corte Ingles 62-63, 176-177
credit cards 186
crime 187
customs regulations 185

D

Decorative Arts Museum 152-153
Domenich i Montaner, Lluis 94,
   123, 125
Dragon without St George (Nagel)
   37
Drassanes 16, 20-23
dress code 184-185
driving 185

E

L'Eixample 110-141
   Casa Milà 112, 114-117
   entertainment 181
   Fundació Antoni Tàpies 118
   Fundació Francisco Godia 119
   Gràcia 112, 120-121
   Hospital de la Santa Creu i Sant
      Pau 122-123
   hotels 165
   Manzana de la Discordia 112,
      124-127
   map 113
   Museu del la Musica 128
   Museu del Perfum 129
   Parc Güell 112, 130-133
   Parc del Laberint 134-135
   Plaça Catalunya 112
   restaurants 170-171
   Sagrada Familia 136-141
   shopping 176-177
   walk 112

electricity 185
embassies and consulates
   185
entertainment 178-181
Església de la Mercè 49, 64
espadrilles 174
Espai Gaudí 117
Estadí Olímpic 29
Ethnology Museum 29

F

FC Barcelona 150-151
Festa Major 121
festivals and events 9, 121, 184
flea market 177
Font de Canaletes 75
Font Màgica 16, 42
Font Monumental 42
football 150-151
Fran Daurel Foundation 40
Francisco Godia Foundation
   119
Frederic Mares Museum 46, 51,
   58-59
Fundació Antoni Tàpies 118
Fundació Francisco Godia 119
Fundació Joan Miró 16, 24-25
funiculars 19, 145, 155

G

Ganchegui, Luis Pena 37
Ganiveteria Roca 65
gardens and parks
   Jardí Botanic 26-27
   Jardíns Cinto Verdaguer 28
   Jardíns Laribal 28
   Jardíns Mossen Costa i Llobera
      28
   Parc d'Attraccions de Tibidabo
      154-155
   Parc de la Ciutadella 80, 96-97
   Parc de l'Espanya Industrial
      37
   Parc Güell 112, 130-133
   Parc de Joan Miro 37
   Parc del Laberint 134-135
   Parc Zoologic 98
Gaudí, Antoni 70, 96, 152
   Casa Battló 114, 125, 126
   Casa Milà 112, 114-117
   Palau Güell 60-61
   Parc Güell 112, 130-133
   Sagrada Familia 136-141
Gehry, Frank 8, 83, 100
Generalitat 72, 73
Golden Fish (Gehry) 83
Golondrina pleasure boats
   102-103
Gothic Quarter see Barri Gòtic
Gràcia 112, 120-121
Gran Teatre del Liceu 77, 180

Spotlight On Barcelona

Acknowledgements

The Automobile Association would like to thank the following photographers, companies and picture libraries for their assistance in the preparation of this book.

Front cover (across from top left, a-k):
(a)Fans, Barri Gotic, AA/S Day; (b)Palau Sant Jordi stadium, AA/S Day; (c)Cathedral interior, AA/S Day; (d)Fountains, Placa de Catalonia, AA/S Day; (e)Façade, Placa da Catalonia, AA/S Day; (f)b/g La Sagrada Familia, AA/S Day; (g)Finca Guell, AA/S Day; (h)La Boqueria market, AA/S Day; (i)Casa Batllo, AA/C Garcia; (j)La Sagrada Familia, AA/S Day; (k)Columbus Monument, AA/S Day.

Abbreviations for the picture credits are as follows – (t) top; (b) bottom; (c) centre; (l) left; (r) right; (AA) AA World Travel Library.

3 AA/M Chaplow; 4l AA/M Jourdan; 4c AA/S Day; 4r AA/M Jourdan; 5l AA/S Day; 5c AA/M Jourdan; 5r AA/M Chaplow; 6/7 AA/S Day; 8/9 AA/S Day; 9 AA/S Day; 12t AA/S Day; 12bl AA/M Chaplow; 12br AA/M Jourdan; 13tl AA/P Wood; 13tr AA/P Wilson; 13b AA/M Jourdan; 14t AA/P Wilson; 14b AA/M Jourdan; 15 AA/M Chaplow; 16t AA/M Jourdan; 16tc AA/P Wilson; 16c AA/S Day; 16bc AA/M Jourdan; 16b AA/S Day; 18 AA/S Day; 19 AA/M Jourdan; 20 AA/M Jourdan; 21 AA/P Wilson; 22/23t AA/M Jourdan; 22/23b AA/M Jourdan; 23 AA/M Jourdan; 24/25 AA/S Day; 25 AA/S Day (© Succession Miro/ADAGP, Paris and DACS London, 2007); 26 AA/M Chaplow; 27 AA/J Tims; 28/29 AA/M Chaplow; 30/31 AA/M Chaplow; 31 AA/M Jourdan; 32 AA/M Jourdan; 33 AA/M Jourdan; 34 AA/M Jourdan; 35l AA/M Jourdan; 35r AA/M Jourdan; 36 AA/S Day; 37 AA/M Jourdan; 38 AA/M Jourdan; 39 AA/S Day; 40/41 AA/M Jourdan; 41 AA/M Jourdan; 42 AA/M Jourdan; 43 AA/S Day; 44t AA/M Jourdan; 44b AA/M Chaplow; 45 AA/S McBride; 46t AA/M Jourdan; 46tc AA/P Wilson; 46c AA/P Wilson; 46bc AA/M Jourdan; 46b AA/M Chaplow; 48 AA/M Chaplow; 49 AA/M Chaplow; 50 AA/M Chaplow; 51t AA/M Chaplow; 51b AA/M Chaplow; 52 AA/M Jourdan; 53 AA/M Jourdan; 54 AA/M Jourdan; 54/55 AA/M Jourdan; 55 AA/S Day; 56 AA/P Wilson; 57 AA/P Wilson; 58 AA/P Wilson; 59 AA/S Day; 60 AA/M Jourdan; 61 AA/M Jourdan; 62/63 Kevin Foy/Alamy; 63 PhotoBliss/Alamy; 64 AA/M Jourdan; 65 AA/M Chaplow; 66 AA/M Jourdan; 67 AA/M Jourdan; 68 AA/M Jourdan; 68/69 AA/S Day; 70/71 AA/S Day; 72 AA/M Chaplow; 72/73 AA/M Chaplow; 74 AA/S Day; 75 AA/S Day; 76 AA/M Jourdan; 76/77 AA/M Jourdan; 77 AA/M Chaplow; 78t AA/M Chaplow; 78b AA/M Chaplow; 79 AA/M Chaplow; 80t AA/M Jourdan; 80tc Rough Guides/Alamy; 80c AA/M Chaplow; 80bc AA/M Jourdan; 80b AA/P Wilson; 82 AA/M Jourdan; 83 AA/M Jourdan; 84l AA/M Jourdan; 84r AA/M Jourdan; 85 AA/M Jourdan; 86 AA/M Chaplow; 87 AA/M Chaplow; 88 Rough Guides/Alamy; 89 Rough Guides/Alamy; 90/91 AA/S Day; 92 AA/M Jourdan; 93t travelstock44/Alamy; 93b AA/M Jourdan; 94/95 AA/M Chaplow; 95 AA/M Jourdan; 96 AA/P Wilson; 97 AA/S Day; 98 AA/P Wilson; 99 AA/M Jourdan; 100/101 AA/M Jourdan; 102/103 AA/M Jourdan; 104 AA/S McBride; 105t AA/M Jourdan; 105b AA/M Jourdan; 106/107 AA/P Wilson; 107 AA/S Day; 108 AA/P Wilson; 109l AA/M Chaplow; 109r AA/M Jourdan; 110t AA/M Jourdan; 110b AA/M Jourdan; 111 AA/S Day; 112t AA/M Chaplow; 112tc AA/P Wilson; 112c AA/M Jourdan; 112bc AA/M Chaplow; 112b AA/M Jourdan; 114/115 AA/M Jourdan; 116 AA/S Day; 116/117 AA/S Day; 117 AA/M Jourdan; 118 AA/M Jourdan; 119 Godofoto.net; 120/121 AA/M Chaplow; 122 AA/M Jourdan; 123 AA/M Jourdan; 124 AA/P Wilson; 125 AA/C Garcia; 126 AA/C Garcia; 127 AA/M Chaplow; 128 AA/S McBride; 129 Rough Guides/Alamy; 130 AA/M Jourdan; 131 AA/M Jourdan; 132 AA/M Jourdan; 132/133 AA/M Jourdan; 133 AA/M Jourdan; 134/135 AA/M Chaplow; 136 AA/M Jourdan; 137 AA/M Chaplow; 138 AA/M Chaplow; 139 AA/S Day; 140 AA/M Chaplow; 141 AA/M Jourdan; 142t AA/M Jourdan; 142b AA/D Day; 143 AA/M Jourdan; 144/145 AA/P Wilson; 146 AA/P Enticknap; 147 AA/S Watkins; 148 Toni Vilches/Alamy; 149 Toni Vilches/Alamy; 150 AA/M Jourdan; 150/151 AA/M Jourdan; 152/153 AA/M Chaplow; 153 AA/M Chaplow; 154/155 AA/P Enticknap; 156 AA/P Wilson; 157 AA/M Chaplow; 158 AA/P Enticknap; 159 AA/P Enticknap; 160 AA/S McBride; 161 AA/M Jourdan; 162 AA/S McBride; 166 AA/S McBride; 172 AA/M Chaplow; 178 AA/M Jourdan; 182 AA/S Day; 183 AA/M Jourdan; 184 AA/P Enticknap; 187 AA/M Jourdan; 188 AA/M Chaplow.

Every effort has been made to trace the copyright holders, and we apologise in advance for any accidental errors. We would be happy to apply the corrections in the following edition of this publication.

The Automobile Association would like to thank all other contributors to this publication.